Research Report on the Development of Star-rated Hotels in China（2018）

中国星级饭店
行业发展研究报告
2018

中华人民共和国文化和旅游部市场管理司　编

中国旅游出版社

目　录

Part I　发展现状与特征分析

第一章 2017 年度我国星级饭店行业发展总体特征 …………………… 2

一、星级饭店行业规模稳中有变 ………………………………… 2

二、星级饭店整体盈利能力大幅提升 …………………………… 3

三、各星级饭店经营业绩表现差异 ……………………………… 3

四、星级饭店各季度发展稳中有进 ……………………………… 4

五、星级饭店区域发展不均衡 …………………………………… 5

第二章 我国星级饭店行业规模及经营情况 …………………………… 7

一、规模及结构 …………………………………………………… 7

二、营业收入 ……………………………………………………… 11

三、利润总额 ……………………………………………………… 19

四、平均出租率 …………………………………………………… 21

五、平均房价 ……………………………………………………… 23

六、人力资源情况 ………………………………………………… 25

第三章 我国星级饭店季度统计分析 …………………………………… 29

一、2017 年各季度我国星级饭店整体情况 …………………… 29

二、2017 年第一季度我国星级饭店市场研究 ……………………… 31

三、2017 年第二季度我国星级饭店市场研究 ……………………… 33

四、2017 年第三季度我国星级饭店市场研究 ……………………… 36

五、2017 年第四季度我国星级饭店市场研究 ……………………… 38

第四章　我国星级饭店区域市场分析 ……………………… 41

一、2017 年度我国星级饭店区域市场整体情况 …………………… 41

二、华北地区行业分析（北京、天津、河北、山西和内蒙古）………… 47

三、东北地区行业分析（黑龙江、吉林和辽宁）………………………… 53

四、华东地区行业分析（上海、江苏、浙江、安徽、福建和山东）……… 59

五、华南地区行业分析（广东、广西和海南）…………………………… 66

六、华中地区行业分析（江西、河南、湖北和湖南）…………………… 72

七、西南地区行业分析（重庆、四川、贵州、云南和西藏）…………… 78

八、西北地区行业分析（陕西、甘肃、青海、宁夏和新疆）…………… 85

Part II　Current Situation and Characteristics Analysis

Chapter I　The General Characteristics for the Development of China's Star-rated Hotels in 2017 ……………………………… 94

I.　Stable Changing of Star-rated Hotel Industry Scale …………………… 94

II.　Significant Improvement in Overall Profitability ……………… 95

III.　Different Performances of All Star-rated Hotels ……………… 96

IV.　Steady Progress in Quarterly Development of Star-rated Hotels ………… 98

V.　Imbalanced Regional Development of Star-rated Hotels ………………… 98

Chapter II The Scale and Operation of China's Star-rated Hotels ········ 101

    I.   Scale and Composition ·· 101

    II.   Operational Revenues·· 106

    III. Total Profits···116

    IV. Average Occupancy Rate (AOR) ···118

    V.   Average Daily Rate (ADR)··· 120

    VI. Human Resources ··· 122

Chapter III Quarterly Statistical Analysis of Star-rated Hotels in China ··· 127

    I.   Overall Quarterly Situation of Star-rated Hotels in China, 2017············ 127

    II.   Research on China's Star-rated Hotels Market: Q1 2017 ··················· 130

    III. Research on China's Star-rated Hotels Market: Q2 2017 ··················· 133

    IV. Research on China's Star-rated Hotels Market: Q3 2017 ··················· 135

    V.   Research on China's Star-rated Hotels Market: Q4 2017 ··················· 138

Chapter IV Analysis of the Regional Market of China's Star-rated Hotel

               Industry ··· 142

    I.   Overall Situation of Regional Market of China's Star-rated Hotels in

        2017 ··· 142

    II.   Analysis of Star-rated Hotel Industry in North China (Beijing, Tianjin, Hebei,

        Shanxi and Inner Mongolia) ·· 149

    III. Analysis of Star-rated Hotel Industry in Northeast China (Heilongjiang, Jilin

        and Liaoning) ·· 157

    IV. Analysis of Star-rated Hotel Industry in East China (Shanghai, Jiangsu,

        Zhejiang, Anhui, Fujian and Shandong)······································ 164

    V.   Analysis of Star-rated Hotel Industry in South China (Guangdong, Guangxi

        and Hainan)··· 172

    VI. Analysis of Star-rated Hotel Industry in Central China (Jiangxi, Henan,

       Hubei and Hunan) ·· 179

VII. Analysis of Star-rated Hotel Industry in Southwest China (Chongqing,
       Sichuan, Guizhou, Yunnan and Tibet) ······················· 187

VIII. Analysis of Star-rated Hotel Industry in Northwest China (Shaanxi, Gansu,
       Qinghai, Ningxia and Xinjiang) ······························· 195

Part I
发展现状与特征分析

2017 年度我国星级饭店行业发展总体特征

本报告数据来源于国家文化和旅游部发布的统计公报，其中第一、第二和第四章的内容采用全国星级饭店统计年报，第三章的内容采用全国星级饭店统计季报。

《2017 年度全国星级饭店统计公报》显示，截至 2017 年底，全国共有 10645 家星级饭店，其中 10417 家在全国星级饭店统计调查管理系统中完成了经营数据的填报，最终有 9566 家星级饭店的数据通过了省级旅游主管部门的审核。根据这些通过审核的数据，2017 年度我国星级饭店呈现出以下特征：

一、星级饭店行业规模稳中有变

基于供给侧结构性改革、住宿业态不断丰富、行业投资更趋理性以及星级饭店自身结构性调整，与 2016 年相比，2017 年星级饭店行业规模稳中有变，具体表现为：星级饭店数量同比减少 295 家，降幅为 2.99%；客房数量为 147.06 万间 / 套，同比增幅为 3.53%；床位数为 250.55 万张，同比增幅为 0.91%；固定资产规模为 5161.10 亿元，同比降幅为 0.26%；内资饭店在投资主体中占据比例为 96.08%，同比降幅为 8.00%。

从星级结构看，四星级和五星级饭店数量呈增长趋势，一星级至三星级饭店数量呈下降趋势。具体表现为：2017 年四星级和五星级饭店数量分别为 2412 家和 816 家，同比增幅为 2.07% 和 2.00%；一星级至三星级饭店数量分别为 64 家、1660 家和 4614 家，同比降幅为 9.86%、6.27% 和 4.98%。

从各星级饭店占比看，三星级饭店数量占比最高，四星级和五星级饭店数量占比逐年上升，一星级和二星级饭店数量占比逐年下降。具体表现为：2017 年三星级、四星级、二星级、五星级和一星级饭店数量占比分别为 48.23%、25.21%、17.35%、8.53% 和 0.67%，四星级和五星级饭店占比同比增幅分别为 5.22% 和 5.18%，一星级至三星级饭店占比同比降幅分别为 6.94%、3.40% 和 2.05%。

二、星级饭店整体盈利能力大幅提升

基于顾客消费能力的增强、营业税改增值税的效应、信息技术的进步以及星级饭店自身经营管理能力的提升，与 2016 年相比，2017 年星级饭店主要经营指标整体表现为发展态势良好，盈利能力大幅提升。其中，利润总额为 72.47 亿元，同比增幅为 1438.64%；营业收入为 2083.93 亿元，同比增幅为 2.80%；百元固定资产实现营业收入为 40.38 元，同比增幅为 3.06%；每间客房实现营业收入为 14.17 万元，同比降幅为 0.70%；平均出租率为 54.80%，同比增幅为 0.13%；平均房价为 343.43 元/间·夜，同比增幅为 2.66%；从业人员数量为 112.41 万人，同比降幅为 6.06%；人房比为 0.76 人/间，同比降幅为 9.26%。

三、各星级饭店经营业绩表现差异

2017 年度，各星级饭店在主要经营指标上表现出不同的特点和趋势。

从利润总额看，二星级至五星级饭店呈增长趋势，一星级饭店呈下降趋势。具体来看，二星级至五星级饭店利润总额分别为 1.78 亿元、1.85 亿元、3.20 亿元和 65.57 亿元，同比增幅分别为 11.25%、108.96%、114.70% 和 44.59%；一星级饭店利润总额为 0.07 亿元，同比降幅为 58.82%。

从营业收入看，二星级、四星级和五星级饭店呈增长趋势，一星级和三星级饭店呈下降趋势。具体来看，二星级、四星级和五星级饭店营业收入分别为 78.55 亿元、714.91 亿元和 812.71 亿元，同比增幅分别为 4.21%、1.57% 和 6.42%；一星级和三星级饭店营业收入分别为 1.13 亿元和 476.43 亿元，同比降幅分别为 2.59% 和 1.39%。

从百元固定资产实现营业收入看，一星级至三星级饭店呈增长趋势，四星级和五星级饭店呈下降趋势。具体来看，一星级至三星级饭店百元固定资产实现营业收入分别为 73.40 元、42.94 元和 46.76 元，同比增幅分别为 53.11%、58.33% 和 2.36%；四星级和五星级饭店百元固定资产实现营业收入分别为 37.05 元和 40.08 元，同比降幅分别为 4.51% 和 6.14%。

从每间客房实现营业收入看，一星级、二星级和五星级饭店呈增长趋势，三星级和四星级饭店呈下降趋势。具体来看，一星级、二星级和五星级饭店每间客房实现营业收入分别为 3.72 万元、6.31 万元和 28.38 万元，同比增幅分别为 1.09%、3.61% 和 2.10%；三星级和四星级饭店每间客房实现营业收入分别为 37.05 万元和 14.19 万元，同比降幅分别为 4.51% 和 5.21%。

从平均出租率看，一星级、四星级和五星级饭店呈增长趋势，二星级和三星级饭店呈下降趋势。具体来看，一星级、四星级和五星级饭店平均出租率分别为 52.62%、56.63% 和 61.43%，同比增幅分别为 0.84%、1.82% 和 4.88%；二星级和三星级饭店平均出租率分别为 47.08% 和 51.30%，同比降幅分别为 10.10% 和 2.32%。

从平均房价看，一星级至三星级饭店呈增长趋势，四星级和五星级饭店呈下降趋势。具体来看，一星级至三星级饭店平均房价分别为 102.39 元 / 间·夜、171.17 元 / 间·夜和 220.36 元 / 间·夜，同比增幅分别为 1.99%、9.96% 和 5.11%；四星级和五星级饭店平均房价分别为 328.06 元 / 间·夜和 612.35 元 / 间·夜，同比降幅分别为 1.39% 和 2.22%。

从从业人员数量看，一星级、三星级至五星级饭店呈下降趋势，二星级饭店呈增长趋势。具体来看，一星级、三星级至五星级饭店从业人员分别为 0.12 万人、34.64 万人、41.77 万人和 29.72 万人，同比降幅分别为 9.09%、12.70%、3.31% 和 1.75%；二星级饭店从业人员为 6.16 万人，同比增幅为 0.33%。

从人房比看，二星级至五星级饭店呈下降趋势，一星级饭店呈增长趋势。具体来看，二星级至五星级饭店人房比分别为 0.49 人 / 间、0.63 人 / 间、0.83 人 / 间和 1.04 人 / 间，同比降幅分别为 2.00%、12.50%、9.78% 和 5.45%；一星级饭店人房比为 0.40 人 / 间，同比增幅为 14.29%。

四、星级饭店各季度发展稳中有进

2017 年第一至第四季度，星级饭店在主要经营指标上表现为稳中有进。

从营业收入看，第一至第四季度稳步上升，从第一季度营业收入 476.21 亿元，增至第四季度的 577.70 亿元，增加了 101.49 亿元，增幅为 21.31%。

从每间可供出租客房收入看，第一至第三季度稳步攀升，第四季度小幅回稳。具体来看，第一至第四季度分别为 170.60 元 / 间·夜、187.40 元 / 间·夜、206.12 元 / 间·夜和 203.28 元 / 间·夜，同比增幅分别为 4.04%、3.86%、7.63% 和 5.29%。

从平均出租率看，和每间可供出租客房收入表现规律类似，第一至第三季度稳步攀升，第四季度小幅回稳。具体来看，第一至第四季度平均出租率分别为 50.20%、56.19%、60.58 和 57.71%，同比增幅分别为 2.57%、1.61%、3.50% 和 1.96%。

从平均房价看，第一至第四季度平均房价分别为 339.87 元 / 间·夜、333.50 元 / 间·夜、340.25 元 / 间·夜和 352.23 元 / 间·夜，同比增幅分别为 1.44%、2.21%、4.00% 和 3.25%。

五、星级饭店区域发展不均衡

2017 年度，星级饭店各区域市场在主要经营指标上发展不均衡。

从数量分布看，华东地区数量最多，为 2508 家，占全国星级饭店总数的比例为 26.22%；东北地区数量最少，为 638 家，占比 6.67%；其次为华中、华北、西南、西北和华南地区，数量分别为 1400 家、1359 家、1331 家、1182 家和 1148 家，占比分别为 14.64%、14.21%、13.91%、12.36% 和 12.00%。

从利润总额看，华东地区盈利最多，为 48.85 亿元；其次是华南、华中、华北和西南地区，分别盈利 25.07 亿元、3.46 亿元、2.43 亿元和 0.26 亿元；东北和西北地区分别亏损 4.93 亿元和 2.68 亿元。

从营业收入看，华东地收入最多，为 814.56 亿元，占全国星级饭店收入总额的比例为 39.09%；东北地区收入最少，为 81.30 亿元，占比为 3.90%；其次为华北、华南、华中、西南和西北地区，营业收入分别为 396.88 亿元、294.01 亿元、203.18 亿元、175.25 亿元和 118.75 亿元，占比分别为 19.04%、14.11%、9.75%、8.41% 和 5.70%。

从百元固定资产实现营业收入看，华东地区最多，为 48.14 元；东北地区最少，为 29.39 元；其次分别为华南、华中、华北、西北和西南，百元固定资产实现营业收入分别为 45.83 元、42.09 元、33.78 元、33.16 元和 32.76 元。

从每间客房实现营业收入看，华东地区最多，为 19.71 万元；西北地区最少，为 8.40 万元；其次为华南、华北、华中、西南和东北，每间客房实现营业收入分别为 15.46 万元、13.91 万元、10.71 万元、10.60 万元和 9.50 万元。

从从业人员数量看，华东地区最多，为 36.71 万人；东北地区最少，为 5.58 万人；其次为华北、华南、华中、西南和西北地区，从业人员分别为 18.79 万人、15.51 万人、14.48 万人、12.60 万人和 8.80 万人。

从人房比看，华东地区最多，为 0.89 人 / 间；西北地区最少，为 0.62 人 / 间；其次为华南、华中、西南、华北和东北地区，人房比分别为 0.82 人 / 间、0.76 人 / 间、0.76 人 / 间、0.66 人 / 间和 0.65 人 / 间。

我国星级饭店行业规模及经营情况

一、规模及结构

1. 行业规模

（1）星级饭店数量

2010~2017 年，除 2013 年星级饭店数量有所回升外，全国星级饭店数量整体呈下降趋势，从 2010 年的 11779 家降至 2017 年的 9566 家，星级饭店数量共减少 2213 家，降幅为 18.79%（图 2-1）。

与 2016 年相比，2017 年星级饭店数量同比降幅为 2.99%。

图 2-1　2010~2017 年星级饭店数量及同比变化情况

（2）客房数量

2010~2017 年，全国星级饭店客房数量呈曲线波动，从 2010 年的 147.64 万间 /套到 2017 年的 147.06 万间 / 套，客房数量共减少 0.58 万间 / 套，降幅为 0.39%。与上文中星级饭店数量降幅 18.79% 相比，客房数量变化幅度小于饭店数量变化幅度，反映出平均单个星级饭店客房规模有一定增长（图 2-2）。

与 2016 年相比，2017 年星级饭店客房数量同比增幅为 3.53%。

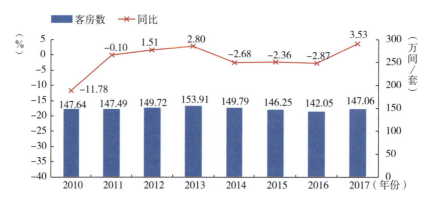

图 2-2　2010~2017 年星级饭店客房数及同比变化情况

（3）床位数

2010~2017 年，全国星级饭店床位数和客房数量表现规律相似，也呈现曲线波动，从 2010 年的 256.64 万张到 2017 年的 250.55 万张，客房数量共减少 6.09 万张，降幅为 2.37%（图 2-3）。

图 2-3　2010~2017 年星级饭店床位数及同比变化情况

与 2016 年相比，2017 年星级饭店床位数同比增幅为 0.91%。

（4）固定资产规模

2010~2015 年，全国星级饭店固定资产规模整体呈现增长趋势，从 2010 年的 4546.77 亿元增加到 2015 年的 5461.30 亿元，固定资产规模共增加 914.53 亿元，增幅为 20.11%。2015~2017 年间，固定资产规模开始呈现下降趋势，2016 年同比降幅为 5.25%，2017 年同比降幅为 0.26%（图 2-4）。

图 2-4 2010~2017 年星级饭店固定资产规模及同比变化情况

2. 星级结构

2010~2017 年，四星级和五星级饭店数量整体呈现增长趋势，四星级饭店数量从 2010 年的 2002 家增加到 2017 年的 2412 家，共增加 410 家，增幅为 20.48%；五星级饭店数量从 2010 年的 545 家增加到 2017 年的 816 家，共增加 271 家，增幅为 49.72%。一星级至三星级饭店数量整体呈现下降趋势，一星级饭店数量从 2010 年的 212 家减少到 2017 年的 64 家，共减少 148 家，降幅为 69.81%；二星级饭店数量从 2010 年的 3636 家减少到 2017 年的 1660 家，共减少 1976 家，降幅为 54.35%；三星级饭店数量从 2010 年的 5384 家减少到 2017 年的 4614 家，共减少 770 家，降幅为 14.30%（表 2-1）。

表 2-1 2010~2017 年各星级饭店数量构成及同比变化情况

年份	五星级		四星级		三星级		二星级		一星级	
	数量（家）	同比（%）	数量（家）	同比（%）	数量（家）	同比（%）	数量（家）	同比（%）	数量（家）	同比（%）
2010	545	7.71	2002	0.91	5384	−9.01	3636	−32.35	212	−53.41
2011	615	12.84	2148	7.29	5473	1.65	3276	−9.9	164	−22.64
2012	640	4.07	2186	1.77	5379	−1.72	3020	−7.81	142	−13.41
2013	739	15.47	2361	8.01	5631	4.68	2831	−6.26	125	−11.97
2014	745	0.81	2373	0.51	5406	−4	2557	−9.68	99	−20.8
2015	789	5.91	2375	0.08	5098	−5.7	2197	−14.03	91	−8.08
2016	800	1.39	2363	−0.51	4856	−4.75	1771	−19.39	71	−21.98
2017	816	2.00	2412	2.07	4614	−4.98	1660	−6.27	64	−9.86

从各星级饭店占比看，2010~2017 年，三星级饭店数量占全国星级饭店数量的比例最高，一星级和二星级饭店数量占比呈逐年下降趋势，四星级和五星级饭店数量占比呈逐年上升趋势（图 2-5）。

图 2-5 2010~2017 年各星级饭店占比情况

2017 年，三星级饭店数量占比为 48.23%，其次为四星级饭店，占比为 25.21%，二星级饭店占比为 17.35%，五星级饭店占比为 8.53%，一星级饭店占比为 0.67%。

3. 投资主体结构

从星级饭店投资主体结构看，2010~2017 年，内资饭店在投资主体中一直占据主力地位，港澳台和外商投资饭店数量整体呈现下降趋势，分别从 2010 年的 298 家和 274 家减少到 2017 年的 197 家和 178 家，分别减少 101 家与 96 家，降幅为 33.89% 与 35.04%（图 2-6）。

图 2-6　2010~2017 年星级饭店投资主体结构变化情况

二、营业收入

1. 营业收入及构成

（1）整体星级饭店营业收入

2010~2017 年，全国星级饭店营业收入分别以 2012 年和 2016 年为拐点呈现先增长后下降然后再增长的曲线波动，营业收入从 2010 年的 2122.66 亿元减少到 2017 年的 2083.93 亿元，共减少 38.73 亿元，降幅为 1.82%。营业收入在 2010~2012 年处于高速增长期，2012 年达到峰值，为 2430.22 亿元；2013~2016 年，受政策影响，营业收入开始下降，且 2014 年降幅最大，为 6.17%；2017 年营业收入同比增长 56.67 亿元，增幅为 2.80%（图 2-7）。

图 2-7　2010~2017 年星级饭店营业收入及同比变化情况

（2）整体星级饭店营业收入构成

2010~2017 年，除 2012 年以外，全国星级饭店客房占营业收入比重都高于餐饮，尤其是在 2013 年以后，客房占营业收入的比重逐年增加，餐饮占营业收入的比重逐年减少（图 2-8）。

2017 年，全国星级饭店客房占营业收入比重为 45.20%，餐饮占营业收入比重为 40.32%，与 2016 年相比，客房占营业收入比重增幅为 0.92%，餐饮降幅为 2.37%。

图 2-8　2010~2017 年星级饭店营业收入构成及变化情况

（3）各星级饭店营业收入及构成

2010~2017 年，全国五星级饭店营业收入虽有小幅波动，但整体仍呈现增长趋势，从 2010 年的 627.12 亿元增长到 2017 年的 812.71 亿元，共增加 185.59 亿元，增幅为 29.59%，客房占营业收入比重都高于餐饮占营业收入比重（图 2-9）。

图 2-9　2010~2017 年五星级饭店营业收入及构成变化情况

2010~2017 年，全国四星级饭店营业收入分别以 2012 年和 2016 年为拐点呈现先增长然后减少然后再增长的曲线波动。客房占营业收入比重在 2013 年之前都低于餐饮占营业收入比重，在 2013 年之后则都高于餐饮占营业收入比重（图 2-10）。

图 2-10　2010~2017 年四星级饭店营业收入及构成变化情况

2010~2017 年，全国三星级饭店营业收入以 2012 年为拐点呈现先增长后减少的趋势。除 2017 年以外，客房占营业收入的比重都低于餐饮占营业收入比重（图 2-11）。

图 2-11　2010~2017 年三星级饭店营业收入及构成变化情况

2010~2017 年，全国二星级饭店营业收入整体上呈下降趋势，从 2010 年的 153.99 亿元降到 2017 年的 78.55 亿元，共减少 75.44 亿元，降幅为 48.99%。客房占营业收入的比重都高于餐饮占营业收入比重（图 2-12）。

图 2-12　2010~2017 年二星级饭店营业收入及构成变化情况

2010~2017 年，全国一星级饭店营业收入整体上呈下降趋势，从 2010 年的 3.68 亿元下降到 2017 年的 1.13 亿元，共减少 2.55 亿元，降幅为 69.29%。除 2017 年以外，客房占营业收入的比重都高于餐饮占营业收入比重（图 2-13）。

图 2-13　2010~2017 年一星级饭店营业收入及构成变化情况

2. 百元固定资产实现营业收入

（1）整体星级饭店百元固定资产实现营业收入

2010~2017 年，全国星级饭店百元固定资产实现营业收入分别以 2012 年和 2015 年为拐点呈现先增长然后减少然后再增长的曲线波动，其中，2011 年增幅最大，同比增加 3.78 元，增幅为 8.10%；2013 年降幅最大，同比下降 5.27 元，降幅为 10.34%（因 2009 年全国星级饭店统计公报中未有百元固定资产实现营业收入指标统计信息，故图 2-14 中 2010 年同比数据缺失）。

2017 年全国星级饭店百元固定资产实现营业收入为 40.38 元，与 2016 年相比，同比增加 1.2 元，增幅为 3.06%（图 2-14）。

图 2-14　2010~2017 年星级饭店百元固定资产实现营业收入及同比变化情况

（2）各星级饭店百元固定资产实现营业收入

2010~2017 年，四星级和五星级饭店百元固定资产实现营业收入分别在 2012 年和 2011 年以后呈现持续下降趋势。其中，四星级和五星级饭店都在 2013 年降幅最大，同比分别减少 6.83 元和 3.33 元，降幅分别为 13.33% 和 7.60%（图 2-15）。

2017 年，四星级和五星级饭店百元固定资产实现营业收入分别为 37.05 元和 40.08 元，与 2016 年相比，同比分别减少 1.75 元和 2.32 元，降幅分别为 4.51% 和 6.14%。

图 2-15 2010~2017 年高星级饭店百元固定资产实现营业收入变化情况

2010~2017 年，一星级至三星级饭店百元固定资产实现营业收入都呈现出曲线波动。其中，一星级饭店在 2015 年增幅最大，同比增加 49.29 元，增幅为 127.04%；二星级饭店在 2016 年降幅最大，同比减少 20.31 元，降幅为 42.60%；三星级饭店在 2015 年降幅最大，同比减少 11.76 元，降幅为 24.19%；（图 2-16）。

2017 年，一星级至三星级饭店百元固定资产实现营业收入分别为 73.40 元、42.94 元和 46.76 元，与 2016 年相比，同比分别增加 25.46 元、15.82 元和 1.08 元，增幅分别为 53.11%、58.33% 和 2.36%。

图 2-16　2010~2017 年低星级饭店百元固定资产实现营业收入变化情况

3. 每间客房实现营业收入

（1）整体星级饭店每间客房实现营业收入

2010~2017 年，全国星级饭店每间客房实现营业收入呈现曲线波动。其中，2011 年增幅最大，同比增加 1.32 万元，增幅为 9.18%；2013 年降幅最大，同比下降 1.33 万元，降幅为 8.19%（因 2009 年全国星级饭店统计公报中未有每间客房实现营业收入指标统计信息，故图 2-17 中 2010 年同比数据缺失）。

2017 年全国星级饭店每间客房实现营业收入为 14.17 万元，与 2016 年相比，同比下降 0.1 万元，降幅为 0.70%（图 2-17）。

图 2-17　2010~2017 年星级饭店每间客房实现营业收入及同比变化情况

（2）各星级饭店每间客房实现营业收入

2010~2017 年，四星级饭店每间客房实现营业收入在 2012 年以后呈现持续下降趋势；五星级饭店每间客房实现营业收入呈现曲线波动。其中，四星级饭店在 2013 年降幅最大，同比下降 2.19 万元，降幅为 11.54%；五星级饭店在 2012 年降幅最大，同比减少 3.04 万元，降幅为 9.05%（图 2-18）。

2017 年，四星级饭店每间客房实现营业收入为 14.19 万元，与 2016 年相比，同比减少 0.78 万元，降幅为 5.21%；五星级饭店每间客房实现营业收入为 28.38 万元，同比增加 0.56 万元，增幅为 2.01%。

图 2-18　2010~2017 年高星级饭店每间客房实现营业收入变化情况

2010~2017 年，一星级和二星级饭店每间客房实现营业收入都呈现出曲线波动；三星级饭店在 2012 年以后呈现持续下降趋势。其中，一星级饭店在 2015 年增幅最大，同比增加 1.63 万元，增幅为 43.01%；二星级饭店在 2012 年增幅最大，同比增加 0.63 万元，增幅为 10.08%；三星级饭店在 2013 年降幅最大，同比减少 1.3 万元，降幅为 11.34%（图 2-19）。

2017 年，一星级和二星级饭店百元固定资产实现营业收入分别为 3.72 万元和 6.31 万元，与 2016 年相比，同比分别增加 0.04 万元和 0.22 万元，增幅分别为 1.09% 和 3.61%；三星级饭店百元固定资产实现营业收入为 8.62 万元，同比减少 0.18 万元，降幅为 2.05%。

图 2-19　2010~2017 年低星级饭店每间客房实现营业收入变化情况

三、利润总额

1. 整体星级饭店利润总额

2010~2017 年，全国星级饭店利润总额呈现曲线波动，其中，2013~2015 年星级饭店利润总额表现为亏损，其他年份表现为盈利（因 2009 年全国星级饭店统计公报中未有利润总额指标统计信息，故图 2-20 中 2010 年同比数据缺失）。

因 2016 年 5 月 1 日起国家全面实行营业税改增值税，全国星级饭店利润总额在 2016 年转亏为盈，在 2017 年实现较大增幅，同比增加 67.76 亿元，增幅为 1438.64%（图 2-20）。

图 2-20　2010~2017 年星级饭店利润总额及同比变化情况

2. 各星级饭店利润总额

2010~2017 年，五星级饭店均表现为盈利状态；四星级饭店利润总额呈现曲线波动，其中在 2013~2016 年均表现为亏损（图 2-21）。

2017 年，四星级和五星级饭店利润总额分别为 3.20 亿元和 65.57 亿元，与 2016 年相比，同比分别增加 24.97 亿元和 20.22 亿元，增幅分别为 114.70% 和 44.59%。

图 2-21　2010~2017 年高星级饭店利润总额变化情况

2010~2017 年，一星级和二星级饭店均表现为盈利状态；三星级饭店直到 2017 年才转亏为盈（图 2-22）。

图 2-22　2010~2017 年低星级饭店利润总额变化情况

2017 年，二星级和三星级饭店利润总额分别为 1.78 亿元和 1.85 亿元，与 2016 年相比，同比分别增加 0.18 亿元和 22.49 亿元，增幅分别为 11.25% 和 108.96%；一星级饭店利润总额为 0.07 亿元，同比减少 0.1 亿元，降幅为 58.82%。

四、平均出租率

1. 整体星级饭店平均出租率

图 2-23　2010~2017 年星级饭店平均出租率及同比变化情况

2010~2017 年，全国星级饭店平均出租率分别以 2011 年和 2015 年为拐点呈现先增长然后减少然后再增长的曲线波动，其中，2013 年降幅最大，降幅为 5.87%；2010 年增幅最大，增幅为 4.15%（图 2-23）。

2017 年全国星级饭店平均出租率为 54.80%，与 2016 年相比，增幅为 0.13%。

2. 各星级饭店平均出租率

2010~2017 年，四星级和五星级饭店平均出租率分别以 2011 年和 2015 年为拐点呈现先增长然后减少然后再增长的曲线波动。其中，四星级和五星级饭店均在 2013 年降幅最大，分别为 5.64% 和 6.43%（图 2-24）。

2017 年，四星级和五星级饭店平均出租率分别为 56.63% 和 61.43%，与 2016

21

年相比，增幅分别为 1.82% 和 4.88%。

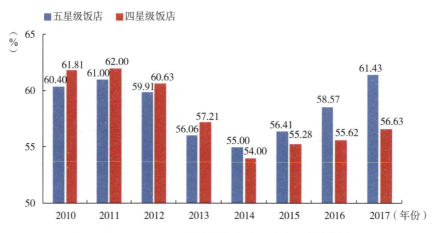

图 2-24　2010~2017 年高星级饭店平均出租率变化情况

2010~2017 年，一星级和二星级饭店平均出租率都呈现曲线波动；三星级饭店则处于持续下降状态（图 2-25）。

2017 年，二星级和三星级饭店平均出租率分别为 47.08% 和 51.30%，与 2016 年相比，同比降幅分别为 10.10% 和 2.32%；一星级饭店平均出租率为 52.62%，同比增幅为 0.84%。

图 2-25　2010~2017 年低星级饭店平均出租率变化情况

五、平均房价

1. 整体星级饭店平均房价

2010~2017 年，除 2016 年外，全国星级饭店平均房价整体呈增长趋势。其中 2011 年增幅最大，同比增加 18.12 元 / 间·夜，增幅为 6.14%（因 2009 年全国星级饭店统计公报中未有平均房价指标统计信息，故图 2-26 中 2010 年同比数据缺失）。

2017 年全国星级饭店平均房价为 343.43 元 / 间·夜，与 2016 年相比，同比增加 8.89 元 / 间·夜，增幅为 2.66%（图 2-26）。

图 2-26　2010~2017 年星级饭店平均房价及同比变化情况

2. 各星级饭店平均房价

2010~2017 年，四星级和五星级饭店平均房价在 2012 年以后均呈现持续下降趋势。其中，四星级饭店在 2015 年降幅最大，同比减少 14.88 元 / 间·夜，降幅为 4.19%；五星级饭店在 2016 年降幅最大，同比减少 29.39 元 / 间·夜，降幅为 4.48%（图 2-27）。

2017 年，四星级饭店平均房价为 328.06 元 / 间·夜，与 2016 年相比，同比减少 4.61 元 / 间·夜，降幅为 1.39%；五星级饭店平均房价为 612.35 元 / 间·夜，同比减少 13.92 元 / 间·夜，降幅为 2.22%。

图 2-27　2010~2017 年高星级饭店平均房价变化情况

2010~2017 年，一星级至三星级饭店平均房价都呈现出曲线波动。其中，一星级饭店在 2016 年降幅最大，同比减少 32.37 元/间·夜，降幅为 24.38%；二星级和三星级饭店均在 2017 年增幅最大，分别增加 15.50 元/间·夜和 10.71 元/间·夜，增幅分别为 9.96% 和 5.11%（图 2-28）。

2017 年，一星级饭店平均房价为 102.39 元/间·夜，与 2016 年相比，同比增加 2.00 元/间·夜，增幅为 1.99%。

图 2-28　2010~2017 年低星级饭店平均房价变化情况

六、人力资源情况

1. 从业人员

（1）整体星级饭店从业人员

2010~2017 年，除 2012 年外，全国星级饭店从业人员数量整体呈下降趋势。其中 2016 年降幅最大，同比减少 14.79 万人，降幅为 11.00%（图 2-29）。

2017 年全国星级饭店从业人员为 112.41 万人，与 2016 年相比，同比减少 7.25 万人，降幅为 6.06%。

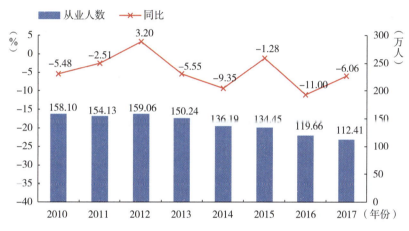

图 2-29　2010~2017 年星级饭店从业人数及同比变化情况

（2）各星级饭店从业人员

2010~2017 年，四星级和五星级饭店从业人员数量分别在 2012 年和 2013 年以后呈现持续下降趋势。其中，四星级和五星级饭店的降副都在 2014 年达到最大值，同比减少 5.50 万人和 2.15 万人，降幅分别为 10.50% 和 6.45%（图 2-30）。

2017 年，四星级饭店从业人数为 41.77 万人，与 2016 年相比，同比减少 1.43 万人，降幅为 3.31%；五星级饭店从业人数为 29.72 万人，同比减少 0.53 万人，降幅为 1.75%。

图 2-30　2010~2017 年高星级饭店从业人员变化情况

2010~2017 年，一星级至三星级饭店从业人员数量都整体表现为下降趋势。其中，一星级饭店从业人员从 2010 年的 0.50 万人下降到 2017 年的 0.12 万人，共减少 0.38 万人，降幅为 76%；二星级饭店从业人员从 2010 年的 17.62 万人到 2017 年的 6.16 万人，共减少 11.46 万人，降幅为 65.04%；三星级饭店从业人员从 2010 年的 59.90 万人下降到 2017 年的 34.64 万人，共减少 25.26 万人，降幅为 42.17%（图 2-31）。

与 2016 年相比，2017 年一星级和二星级饭店从业人员同比增幅分别为 9.09% 和 0.33%；三星级饭店同比降幅为 12.70%。

图 2-31　2010~2017 年低星级饭店从业人员变化情况

2. 人房比

（1）整体星级饭店人房比

2010~2017 年，全国星级饭店人房比整体呈下降趋势，从 2010 年的 1.07 人 / 间下降到 2017 年的 0.76 人 / 间，共减少 0.31 人 / 间，降幅为 28.97%。其中 2017 年降幅最大，同比减少 0.08 人 / 间，降幅为 9.26%（图 2-32）。

图 2-32　2010~2017 年星级饭店人房比及同比变化情况

（2）各星级饭店人房比

2010~2017 年，四星级和五星级饭店人房比都整体表现为下降趋势。其中，四星级饭店人房比从 2010 年的 1.27 人 / 间下降到 2017 年的 0.83 人 / 间，共减少 0.44 人 / 间，降幅为 34.65%；五星级饭店人房比从 2010 年的 1.43 人 / 间到 2017 年的 1.04 人 / 间，共减少 0.39 人 / 间，降幅为 27.27%（图 2-33）。

与 2016 年相比，2017 年四星级和五星级饭店人房比同比降幅分别为 9.78% 和 5.45%。

图 2-33　2010~2017 年高星级饭店人房比变化情况

2010~2017 年，一星级至三星级饭店人房比也都整体呈现下降趋势。其中，一星级饭店人房比从 2010 年的 0.5 人／间下降到 2017 年的 0.4 人／间，共减少 0.1 人／间，降幅为 20%；二星级饭店人房比从 2010 年的 0.71 人／间下降到 2017 年的 0.49 人／间，共减少 0.22 人／间，降幅为 30.99%；三星级饭店人房比从 2010 年的 0.98 人／间下降到 2017 年的 0.63 人／间，共减少 0.35 人／间，降幅为 35.71%（图 2-34）。

与 2016 年相比，2017 年二星级和三星级饭店人房比同比降幅分别为 2% 和 12.50%；一星级饭店人房比同比增幅为 14.29%。

图 2-34 2010~2017 年低星级饭店人房比变化情况

我国星级饭店季度统计分析

2017 年第一季度，国家文化和旅游部全国星级饭店统计调查管理系统（以下称为系统）中有 10782 家星级饭店，完成填报的为 10482 家，填报率为 97.22%；第二季度，系统中有 11607 家星级饭店，完成填报的为 11240 家，填报率为 96.84%；第三季度，系统中有 11492 家星级饭店，完成填报的为 11266 家，填报率为 98.03%；第四季度，系统中有 10962 家星级饭店，完成填报的为 10735 家，填报率为 97.93%。

一、2017 年各季度我国星级饭店整体情况

1. 收入规模及结构

2017 年各季度，全国星级饭店营业收入稳步上升，营业收入从第一季度的 476.21 亿元，增至第四季度的 577.70 亿元，增加 101.49 亿元，增幅为 21.31%。其中，除第一季度比 2016 年同比减少 4.12% 外，其余各季度同比均增加，增幅分别为第二季度 0.39%，第三季度 3.87%，第四季度 6.13%（图 3-1）。

图 3-1　2016 年、2017 年各季度星级饭店收入规模及结构

2017 年，从各季度星级饭店营业收入结构看，除第二季度餐饮收入比重呈现曲线波动外，其他各业务收入占比基本呈现一致走势，客房收入占比从第一季度到第三季度逐步增加，在第四季度回落；餐饮收入占比从第一季度到第三季度逐步减少，在第四季度回升。

2017 年，客房业务收入占全国星级饭店营业收入比重整体呈上升趋势，第一季度、第二季度和第三季度同比增幅分别为 2.95%、1.43% 和 1.65%，第四季度同比减少 2.85%。餐饮业务收入占比整体呈下降趋势，除第二季度同比增幅 12.86% 外，第一季度、第三季度和第四季度同比分别减少 0.51%、3.38% 和 1.39%。

2. 经营情况

2017 年各季度，全国星级饭店平均出租率呈现一致走势，从第一季度到第三季度稳步攀升，在第四季度小幅回稳。2017 年，全国星级饭店平均出租率第一季度最低，为 50.20%，同比增加 1.26 个百分点，增幅为 2.57%；第二季度出租率为 56.19%，同比增加 0.89 个百分点，增幅为 1.61%；第三季度出租率最高，为 60.58%，同比增加 2.05 个百分点，增幅为 3.50%；第四季度出租率为 57.71%，同比增加 1.11 个百分点，增幅为 1.96%（图 3-2）。

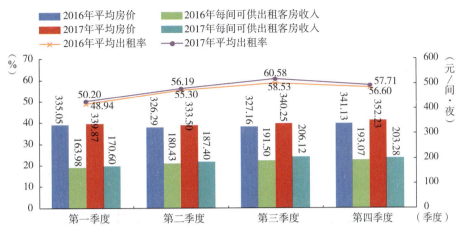

图 3-2　2016 年、2017 年各季度星级饭店经营情况

与 2016 年全国星级饭店第一季度平均房价同比增加、第二至季度第四季度平均房价同比下降的特征不同，2017 年全国星级饭店平均房价各季度均同比增加，分别增加 4.82 元 / 间·夜、7.21 元 / 间·夜、13.09 元 / 间·夜和 11.10 元 / 间·夜，增幅分别为 1.44%、2.21%、4.00% 和 3.25%。

从每间可供出租客房收入看，2017 年各季度，全国星级饭店每间可供出租客房收入与全年出租率变化特征基本一致，呈现稳步增加后回稳的全年总体特征。其中，第一季度最低每间可供出租客房收入，为 170.60 元 / 间·夜；第二季度次之，为 187.40 元 / 间·夜；第三季度、第四季度分别为 206.12 元 / 间·夜、203.28 元 / 间·夜。从变动趋势来看，2017 年各季度每间可供出租客房收入均较 2016 年同比增加，其中第三季度同比差距最大，同比增加 14.62 元 / 间·夜，增幅为 7.63%；第二季度差距最小，同比增加 6.97 元 / 间·夜，增幅为 3.86%。

二、2017 年第一季度我国星级饭店市场研究

1. 收入规模及结构

2017 年第一季度，全国星级饭店实现营业收入 476.21 亿元；其中餐饮收入为 206.19 亿元，占营业收入的 43.30%；客房收入为 209.65 亿元，占营业收入的 44.03%（图 3-3）。

图 3-3　2016 年、2017 年第一季度各星级饭店收入规模及结构

从各星级饭店营业收入看，2017 年第一季度五星级饭店营业收入规模最高，为 184.89 亿元，占全国星级饭店营业收入总额的 38.83%；其次为四星级饭店，共实现营业收入 161.72 亿元，占比 33.96%；三星级饭店共实现营业收入 112.21 亿元，占比 23.56%；一星级、二星级饭店共计实现营业收入 17.38 亿元，合计占比 3.65%。

从各星级饭店营业收入结构看，2017 年第一季度五星级饭店客房收入占比 46.49%，餐饮收入占比 42.21%；四星级饭店客房收入占比 41.95%，餐饮收入占比 43.28%；三星级饭店客房收入占比 42.46%，餐饮收入占比 45.65%；二星级饭店客房收入占比 47.12%，餐饮收入占比 39.74%；一星级饭店客房收入占比 52.53%，餐饮收入占比 43.22%。一星级、二星级和五星级饭店的客房收入占比均超过餐饮收入占比，三星级和四星级饭店的餐饮收入占比超过客房收入占比。与 2016 年同期相比，一星级、四星级和五星级饭店餐饮收入占比均同比下降，分别下降 1.16、0.96 和 1.45 个百分点，降幅分别为 2.61%、2.17% 和 3.32%；二星级和三星级饭店餐饮收入占比均同比增加，分别增加 8.43 和 0.59 个百分点，增幅分别为 26.92% 和 1.31%；各星级饭店客房收入占比均同比增加，一星级到五星级饭店分别增加 0.04、10.42、0.64、0.27 和 1.25 个百分点，增幅分别为 0.08%、28.39%、1.53%、0.65% 和 2.76%。

2. 经营情况

2017 年第一季度，全国星级饭店平均出租率为 50.20%，平均房价为 339.87 元 / 间·夜，每间可供出租客房收入为 170.60 元 / 间·夜。

与 2016 年同期相比，2017 年第一季度全国星级饭店平均出租率增加 1.26 个百分点，增幅为 2.57%，其中五星级饭店增幅最大，增加 2.71 个百分点，增幅为 5.14%；二星级到四星级饭店也都存在不同程度的增加，分别增加 0.50、0.37 和 1.34 个百分点，增幅分别为 1.05%、0.79% 和 2.72%；一星级饭店呈现下降趋势，下降了 1.62 个百分点，降幅为 3.50%。

与 2016 年同期相比，2017 年第一季度全国星级饭店平均房价增加 4.82 元 / 间·夜，增幅为 1.44%，其中五星级饭店呈下降趋势，同比下降 13.85 元 / 间·夜，降幅为 2.18%。

与 2016 年同期相比，2017 年第一季度全国星级饭店每间可供出租客房收入增长 6.62 元 / 间·夜，增幅为 4.04%，其中五星级饭店增幅最大，同比增长 9.53 元 / 间·夜，增幅为 2.84%；二星级到四星级饭店也都有不同程度的增加，同比分别增加 0.68 元 / 间·夜、0.81 元 / 间·夜和 1.94 元 / 间·夜，增幅分别为 0.91%，0.79% 和 1.18%；和平均出租率相同，每间可供出租客房收入也是一星级饭店呈现下降趋势，下降 10.22 元 / 间·夜，降幅为 17.70%（图 3-4）。

图 3-4　2016 年、2017 年第一季度各星级饭店经营情况

三、2017 年第二季度我国星级饭店市场研究

1. 收入规模及结构

2017 年第二季度，全国星级饭店实现营业收入 502.16 亿元，其中餐饮收入

为 232.70 亿元，占营业收入的 46.34%；客房收入为 238.43 亿元，占营业收入的 47.48%（图 3-5）。

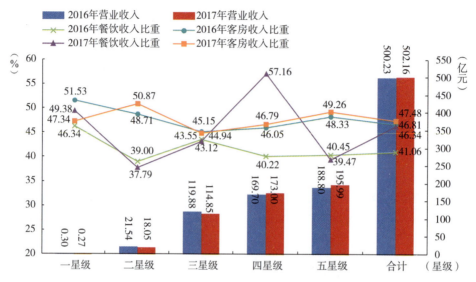

图 3-5　2016 年、2017 年第二季度各星级饭店收入规模及结构

从各星级饭店营业收入看，2017 年第二季度各星级饭店营业收入均较第一季度有所增长，其中五星级饭店第二季度营业收入规模最高，为 195.99 亿元，占全国星级饭店营业收入总额的 39.03%；其次为四星级饭店，共实现营业收入 173.00 亿元，占比 34.45%；三星级饭店共实现营业收入 114.85 亿元，占比 22.87%；一星级、二星级饭店共计实现营业收入 18.32 亿元，合计占比 3.65%。

从各星级饭店营业收入结构看，2017 年第二季度二星级饭店客房收入占比最大，为 50.87%，收入比重差距也最大，客房收入比重超过餐饮收入比重 13.08 个百分点；三星级饭店收入比重差距最小，客房收入比重只超过餐饮收入比重 1.82 个百分点；四星级饭店餐饮收入比重超过客房收入比重 10.37 个百分点；五星级饭店客房收入比重超过餐饮收入比重 9.79 个百分点；各星级饭店平均客房收入比重超过餐饮收入比重 1.14 个百分点。与 2016 年同期相比，客房和餐饮平均收入比重均有所增加，同比增幅分别为 1.43% 和 12.86%，两者之间的差距有所缩小。

2. 经营情况

2017 年第二季度，全国星级饭店平均出租率 56.19%，平均房价 333.50 元 / 间·夜，每间可供出租客房收入 187.40 元 / 间·夜。

与 2016 年同期相比，2017 年第二季度全国星级饭店平均出租率增加了 0.89 个百分点，增幅为 1.61%，其中四星级、五星级饭店均呈现不同程度的增加，同比分别增加 1.71 和 1.93 个百分点，增幅分别为 3.02% 和 3.25%；一星级到三星级饭店呈下降趋势，分别下降了 2.85、1.15 和 0.1 个百分点，降幅分别为 6.27%、2.17% 和 0.19%。

与 2016 年同期相比，2017 年第二季度全国星级饭店平均房价增加了 7.21 元 / 间·夜，增幅为 2.21%，其中二星级和五星级饭店较 2016 年同期均有所增加，分别增加 2.96 元 / 间·夜和 5.11 元 / 间·夜，增幅分别为 1.90% 和 0.84%；一星级、三星级和四星级饭店同比分别下降了 3.73 元 / 间·夜、2.19 元 / 间·夜和 0.72 元 / 间·夜，降幅分别为 3.46%、1.06% 和 0.22%。

与 2016 年同期相比，2017 年第二季度全国星级饭店每间可供出租客房收入增加 6.97 元 / 间·夜，增幅为 3.86%，其中四星级和五星级饭店分别同比增加 5.18 元 / 间·夜和 14.93 元 / 间·夜，增幅分别为 2.79% 和 4.11%；一星级到三星级饭店分别同比下降了 4.67 元 / 间·夜、0.27 元 / 间·夜和 1.35 元 / 间·夜，降幅分别为 9.52%、0.33% 和 1.24%（图 3-6）。

图 3-6　2016 年、2017 年第二季度各星级饭店经营情况

四、2017 年第三季度我国星级饭店市场研究

1. 收入规模及结构

2017 年第三季度，全国星级饭店实现营业收入 538.08 亿元，其中餐饮收入为 206.03 亿元，占营业收入的 38.29%；客房收入为 262.42 亿元，占营业收入的 48.77%（图 3-7）。

图 3-7 2016 年、2017 年第三季度各星级饭店收入规模及结构

从各星级饭店营业收入看，2017 年第三季度，除一星级饭店外，各星级饭店营业收入均较第二季度均有所增长，其中五星级饭店营业收入规模最高，为 204.61 亿元，占全国星级饭店营业收入总额的 38.03%；其次为四星级饭店，共实现营业收入 186.85 亿元，占比 34.73%；三星级饭店共实现营业收入 125.83 亿元，占比 23.38%；一星级、二星级饭店共计实现营业收入 20.79 亿元，合计占比 3.86%。

从各星级饭店营业收入结构看，2017 年第三季度五星级饭店客房收入占比 49.56%，餐饮收入占比 37.99%；四星级饭店客房收入占比 48.13%，餐饮收入占比 37.65%；三星级饭店客房收入占比 47.73%，餐饮收入占比 40.44%；二星级饭店客房收入占比 53.15%，餐饮收入占比 33.98%；一星级饭店客房收入占比 52.21%，餐饮收入占比 43.93%。总体来看，客房收入占比均超过餐饮收入占比。与 2016 年同期相比，一星级到五星级饭店餐饮收入占比均下降，分别下降了 4.57、2.36、1.27、

0.98 和 1.61 个百分点，降幅分别为 9.42%、6.49%、3.04%、2.54% 和 4.07%；各星级饭店客房收入占比均同比增加，一星级到五星级饭店分别增加 1.78、0.37、0.17、0.81 和 1.26 个百分点，增幅分别为 3.53%、0.70%、0.36%、1.71% 和 2.61%。

2. 经营情况

2017 年第三季度，全国星级饭店平均出租率为 60.58%，平均房价 340.25 元 / 间·夜，每间可供出租客房收入 206.12 元 / 间·夜。

与 2016 年同期相比，2017 年第三季度全国星级饭店平均出租率增加了 2.05 个百分点，增幅为 3.50%，其中，五星级饭店同比增长了 2.55 个百分点，增幅为 4.10%；二星级至四星级饭店同比分别增加 2.70、1.00 和 1.57 个百分点，增幅分别为 4.48%、1.77% 和 2.90%；一星级饭店同比下降了 0.37 个百分点，降幅为 0.83%。

与 2016 年同期相比，2017 年第三季度全国星级饭店平均房价增加 13.09 元 / 间·夜，增幅为 4%，其中二星级到五星级饭店同比分别增加 9.08 元 / 间·夜、7.26 元 / 间·夜、1.45 元 / 间·夜和 14.02 元 / 间·夜，增幅分别为 5.41%、3.42%、0.44% 和 2.35%；一星级饭店同比下降 29.19 元 / 间·夜，降幅为 22.86%。

与 2016 年同期相比，2017 年第三季度全国星级饭店每间可供出租客房收入增加 14.62 元 / 间·夜，增幅为 7.63%，其中二星级到五星级饭店同比分别增加 7.68 元 / 间·夜、6.28 元 / 间·夜、9.90 元 / 间·夜和 24.31 元 / 间·夜，增幅分别为 8.47%、5.25%、4.93% 和 6.54%，一星级饭店同比下降 13.37 元 / 间·夜，降幅为 23.50%（图 3-8）。

图 3-8　2016 年、2017 年第三季度各星级饭店经营情况

五、2017年第四季度我国星级饭店市场研究

1. 收入规模及结构

2017年第四季度，全国星级饭店实现营业收入577.70亿元，其中客房收入为252.51亿元，占营业收入的43.71%；餐饮收入为241.65亿元，占营业收入的41.83%（图3-9）。

图3-9 2016年、2017年第四季度各星级饭店收入规模及结构

从各星级饭店营业收入看，2017年第四季度，除一星级和二星级饭店外，各星级饭店营业收入均较第三季度有所增长，其中五星级饭店营业收入规模最高，为232.89亿元，占全国星级饭店营业收入总额的40.31%；其次为四星级饭店，共实现营业收入196.27亿元，占比33.97%；三星级饭店共实现营业收入129.11亿元，占比22.35%；一星级、二星级饭店共计实现营业收入19.43亿元，合计占比3.36%。

从各星级饭店营业收入结构看，2017年第四季度五星级饭店客房收入占比44.53%，餐饮收入占比41.29%；四星级饭店客房收入占比43.12%，餐饮收入占比41.31%；三星级饭店客房收入占比42.65%，餐饮收入占比43.87%；二星级饭店客

房收入占比 47%，餐饮收入占比 39.69%；一星级饭店客房收入占比 40.48%，餐饮收入占比 53.66%。一星级饭店业务重心趋向于餐饮，二星级饭店业务重心趋向于客房，其他星级饭店餐饮、客房收入占比相对均衡。与 2016 年同期相比，一星级、三星级、四星级和五星级饭店餐饮收入占比均同比下降，分别下降 6.58、0.06、0.43 和 1.23 个百分点，降幅分别为 10.92%、0.14%、1.03% 和 2.89%；二星级饭店餐饮收入占比增加，增加 1.76 个百分点，增幅为 4.64%；二星级到五星级饭店客房收入占比均同比下降，分别下降 3.10、0.64、0.67 和 2.09 个百分点，降幅分别为 6.19%、1.48%、1.53% 和 4.48%；一星级饭店客房收入占比增加，增加 4.02 个百分点，增幅为 11.03%。

2. 经营情况

2017 年第四季度，全国星级饭店平均出租率 57.71%，平均房价 352.23 元 / 间·夜，每间可供出租客房收入 203.28 元 / 间·夜。

与 2016 年同期相比，2017 年第四季度全国星级饭店平均出租率增加 1.11 个百分点，增幅为 1.96%，其中五星级饭店同比增加 2.12 个百分点，增幅为 3.44%；一星级、三星级和四星级饭店同比分别增加 0.74、0.26 和 1.08 个百分点，增幅分别为 1.70%、0.49% 和 1.85%；二星级饭店同比下降 2 个百分点，降幅为 3.66%。

与 2016 年同期相比，2017 年第四季度全国星级饭店平均房价增加 11.10 元 / 间·夜，增幅为 3.25%，其中三星级到五星级饭店同比分别增加 5.23 元 / 间·夜、0.71 元 / 间·夜和 19.12 元 / 间·夜，增幅分别为 2.39%、0.21% 和 3.11%；一星级和二星级饭店同比分别下降 12.28 元 / 间·夜和 13.76 元 / 间·夜，降幅分别为 12.04% 和 7.60%。

与 2016 年同期相比，2017 年第四季度全国星级饭店每间可供出租客房收入增加 10.21 元 / 间·夜，增幅为 5.29%，其中三星级到五星级饭店同比分别增加 3.37 元 / 间·夜、4.04 元 / 间·夜和 25.24 元 / 间·夜，增幅分别为 2.88%、2.06% 和 6.67%；一星级和二星级饭店同比分别下降 4.66 元 / 间·夜和 7.43 元 / 间·夜，降幅分别为 10.52% 和 7.95%（图 3-10）。

图 3-10　2016 年、2017 年第四季度各星级饭店经营情况

我国星级饭店区域市场分析

一、2017 年度我国星级饭店区域市场整体情况

1. 数量分布

从 2017 年星级饭店数量分布看，华东地区数量最多，东北地区数量最少。具体来看，华北、东北、华东、华南、华中、西南和西北地区星级饭店数量分别为 1359 家、638 家、2508 家、1148 家、1400 家、1331 家和 1182 家，占全国星级饭店总数的比例分别为 14.21%、6.67%、26.22%、12%、14.64%、13.91% 和 12.36%（图 4-1）。

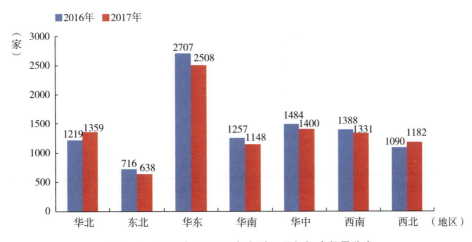

图 4-1　2016 年、2017 年各地区星级饭店数量分布

与 2016 年相比，华北地区数量增幅最大，东北地区数量降幅最大。具体来看，华北和西北星级饭店数量同比分别增加 140 家和 92 家，增幅分别为 11.48% 和 8.44%；东北、华东、华南、华中和西南地区星级饭店数量同比分别减少了 78 家、199 家、109 家、84 家和 57 家，降幅分别为 10.89%、7.35%、8.67%、5.66% 和 4.11%。

2. 营业收入分布

（1）营业收入

从 2017 年星级饭店营业收入看，华东地区收入最多，东北地区收入最少。

具体来看，华北、东北、华东、华南、华中、西南和西北地区星级饭店营业收入分别为 396.88 亿元、81.30 亿元、814.56 亿元、294.01 亿元、203.18 亿元、175.25 亿元和 118.75 亿元，占全国星级饭店收入总数的比例分别为 19.04%、3.90%、39.09%、14.11%、9.75%、8.41% 和 5.70%（图 4-2）。

与 2016 年相比，除华南地区外，其他各地区星级饭店营业收入均呈现上升趋势，其中华北、东北、华东、华中、西南和西北地区星级饭店营业收入同比分别增加 24.44 亿元、1.82 亿元、15.37 亿元、2.57 亿元、9.93 亿元和 3.18 亿元，增幅分别为 6.56%、2.29%、1.92%、1.28%、6.01% 和 2.75%；华南地区营业收入同比减少 0.64 亿元，降幅为 0.22%。

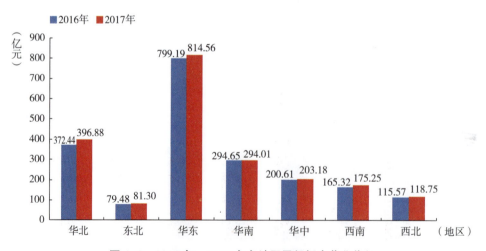

图 4-2　2016 年、2017 年各地区星级饭店营业收入

（2）百元固定资产实现营业收入

2017 年星级饭店百元固定资产实现营业收入以华东地区最多，为 48.14 元；东北地区最少，为 29.39 元；华北、华南、华中、西南和西北地区星级饭店百元固定资产实现营业收入分别为 33.78 元、45.83 元、42.09 元、32.76 元和 33.16 元（图 4-3）。

与 2016 年相比，除华北地区外，其他各地区星级饭店百元固定资产实现营业收入均呈现上升趋势，其中东北、华东、华南、华中、西南和西北地区星级饭店百元固定资产实现营业收入同比分别增加 2.32 元、0.94 元、7.88 元、1.64 元、0.40 元和 0.72 元，增幅分别为 8.57%、1.99%、20.76%、4.05%、1.24% 和 2.22%；华北地区星级饭店百元固定资产实现营业收入减少 1.74 元，降幅为 4.90%。

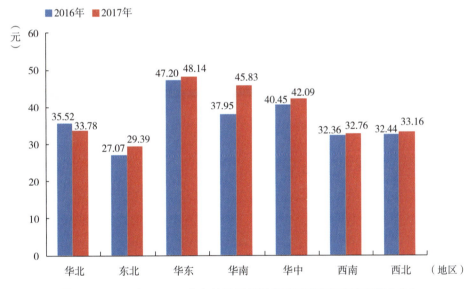

图 4-3　2016 年、2017 年各地区星级饭店百元固定资产实现营业收入

（3）每间客房实现营业收入

2017 年星级饭店每间客房实现营业收入以华东地区最多，为 19.71 万元；西北地区最少，为 8.40 万元；华北、东北、华南、华中和西南地区星级饭店每间客房实现营业收入分别为 13.91 万元、9.50 万元、15.46 万元、10.71 万元和 10.60 万元（图 4-4）。

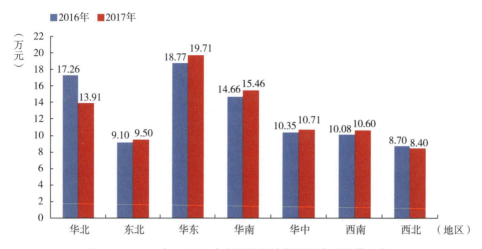

图 4-4　2016 年、2017 年各星级饭店每间客房实现营业收入

与 2016 年相比，除华北和西北地区外，其他各地区星级饭店每间客房实现营业收入均呈现上升趋势。具体来看，东北、华东、华南、华中和西南地区星级饭店每间客房实现营业收入同比分别增加 0.40 万元、0.94 万元、0.80 万元、0.36 万元和 0.52 万元，增幅分别为 4.40%、5.01%、5.46%、3.48% 和 5.16%；华北和西北地区星级饭店每间客房实现营业收入同比分别减少 3.35 万元和 0.30 万元，降幅分别为 19.41% 和 3.45%。

（4）百元营业收入占用固定资产

2017 年星级饭店百元营业收入占用固定资产以东北地区最多，为 340.21 元；华东地区最少，为 207.74 元；华北、华南、华中、西南和西北地区星级饭店百元营业收入占用固定资产分别为 296.04 元、218.19 元、237.59 元、305.28 元和 301.61 元（图 4-5）。

与 2016 年相比，除华北地区外，其他各地区星级饭店百元营业收入占用固定资产均呈现下降趋势。具体来看，东北、华东、华南、华中、西南和西北地区星级饭店百元营业收入占用固定资产同比分别下降 29.20 元、4.10 元、45.29 元、9.64 元、3.79 元和 6.62 元，降幅分别为 7.90%、1.94%、17.19%、3.90%、1.23% 和 2.15%；华北地区星级饭店百元营业收入占用固定资产同比增加 14.54 元，增幅为 5.17%。

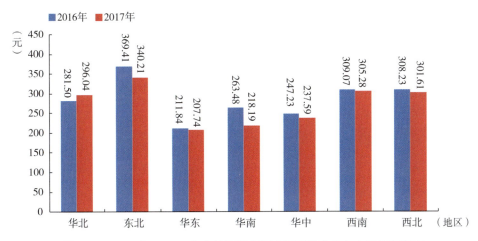

图 4-5　2016 年、2017 年各地区星级饭店百元营业收入占用固定资产

3. 利润总额

2017 年，各地区星级饭店盈利水平差异较大。具体来看，华东地区盈利最多，为 48.85 亿元；其次是华南、华中、华北和西南地区，分别盈利 25.07 亿元、3.46 亿元、2.43 亿元和 0.26 亿元。除上述 5 个地区外，其他地区均有不同程度的亏损，其中东北地区亏损最多，为 4.93 亿元；其次是西北地区，亏损 2.68 亿元（图 4-6）。

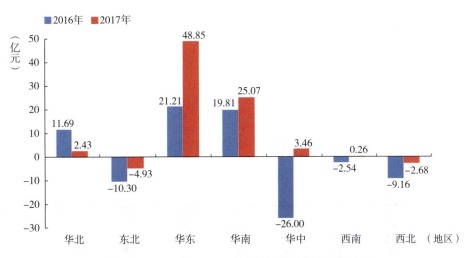

图 4-6　2016 年、2017 年各地区星级饭店利润总额

与 2016 年相比，华中地区变化最大，星级饭店盈利同比增加 29.46 亿元，增

幅为 113.31%；其次是华东地区，星级饭店盈利同比增加 27.64 亿元，增幅为 130.32%；再次分别是西北、东北、华南和西南地区，星级饭店盈利同比分别增加 6.48 亿元、5.37 亿元、5.26 亿元和 2.80 亿元，增幅分别为 70.74%、52.14%、26.55% 和 110.24%。

4. 人力资源情况

2017 年星级饭店从业人数以华东地区最多，为 36.71 万人，同比减少 2.84 万人，降幅为 7.18%；东北地区最少，为 5.58 万人，同比减少 0.50 万人，降幅为 8.22%；华北地区星级饭店从业人数为 18.79 万人，同比增加 0.51 万人，增幅为 2.79%；华南、华中、西南和西北地区星级饭店从业人数分别为 15.51 万人、14.48 万人、12.60 万人和 8.80 万人，同比分别减少 2.13 万人、0.79 万人、0.63 万人和 0.80 万人，降幅分别为 12.07%、5.17%、4.76% 和 8.33%（图 4-7）。

2017 年星级饭店人房比，各地区均呈现不同程度的下降。具体来看，华东地区最多，为 0.89 人/间，同比减少 0.04 人/间，降幅为 4.30%；西北地区最少，为 0.62 人/间，同比减少 0.10 人/间万人，降幅为 13.89%；华北、东北、华南、华中和西南地区星级饭店人房比分别为 0.66 人/间、0.65 人/间、0.82 人/间、0.76 人/间和 0.76 人/间，同比分别减少 0.19 人/间、0.05 人/间、0.06 人/间、0.03 人/间和 0.05 人/间，降幅分别为 22.35%、7.14%、6.82%、3.80% 和 6.17%。

图 4-7　2016 年、2017 年各地区星级饭店从业人数及人房比

二、华北地区行业分析（北京、天津、河北、山西和内蒙古）

1. 数量分布

2017 年度，华北地区星级饭店数量 1359 家，以三星级、四星级饭店为主。具体来看，五星级饭店共计 121 家，占华北地区星级饭店总量的 8.90%；四星级饭店共计 367 家，占华北地区星级饭店总量的 27.01%；三星级饭店共计 566 家，占华北地区星级饭店总量的 41.65%；二星级饭店共计 293 家，占华北地区星级饭店总量的 21.56%；一星级饭店共计 12 家，占华北地区星级饭店总量的 0.88%（图 4-8）。

与 2016 年相比，华北地区五星级饭店占比同比减少 9.55%，四星级饭店占比同比减少 7.79%，三星级饭店占比同比减少 3.48%，二星级饭店占比同比增加 23.39%，一星级饭店占比同比增加 258.79%。

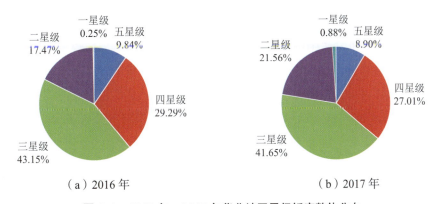

（a）2016 年　　　　　　　　（b）2017 年

图 4-8　2016 年、2017 年华北地区星级饭店整体分布

从星级饭店数量分布来看，2017 年北京星级饭店数量 496 家，占华北星级饭店数量的 36.50%；天津星级饭店数量 80 家，占华北地区星级饭店数量的 5.89%；河北星级饭店数量 338 家，占华北地区星级饭店数量的 24.87%；山西星级饭店数量 203 家，占华北地区星级饭店数量的 14.94%；内蒙古星级饭店数量 242 家，占华北地区星级饭店数量的 17.81%。

与 2016 年相比，北京、山西和内蒙古星级饭店数量同比分别增加 80 家、9 家和 67 家，增幅分别为 19.23%、4.64% 和 38.29%；天津和河北星级饭店数量同比分别减少 4 家和 12 家，降幅分别为 4.76% 和 3.43%（图 4-9）。

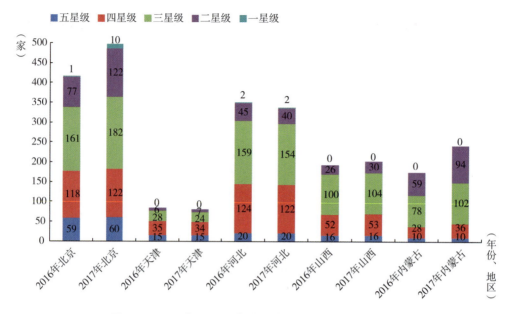

图 4-9 2016 年、2017 年华北地区各星级饭店分布情况

从星级饭店数量分布结构来看，2017 年华北地区三星级饭店占主导地位，其次是四星级、二星级、五星级和一星级饭店。具体来看，北京一星级至五星级饭店数量分别为 10 家、122 家、182 家、122 家和 60 家，占北京市饭店总量的比例分别为 2.02%、24.60%、36.69%、24.60% 和 12.10%；天津一星级至五星级饭店数量分别为 0 家、7 家、24 家、34 家和 15 家，占天津市饭店总量的比例分别为 0%、8.75%、30.00%、42.50% 和 18.75%；河北一星级至五星级饭店数量分别为 2 家、40 家、154 家、122 家和 20 家，占河北省饭店总量的比例分别为 0.59%、11.83%、45.56%、36.09% 和 5.92%；山西一星级至五星级饭店数量分别为 0 家、30 家、104 家、53 家和 16 家，占山西省饭店总量的比例分别为 0%、14.78%、51.23%、26.11% 和 7.88%；内蒙古一星级至五星级饭店数量分别为 0 家、94 家、102 家、36 家和 10 家，占内蒙古自治区饭店总量的比例分别为 0%、38.84%、42.15%、14.88% 和 4.13%。

2. 营业收入分布

（1）营业收入及构成

2017 年华北地区星级饭店实现营业收入 396.88 亿元，同比增加 6.56%，其中实现客房收入 183.75 亿元，占华北地区星级饭店营业收入的 46.30%；餐饮收入

135.56 亿元，占华北地区星级饭店营业收入的 34.16%；其他收入 77.57 亿元，占华北地区星级饭店营业收入的 19.54%（图 4-10）。

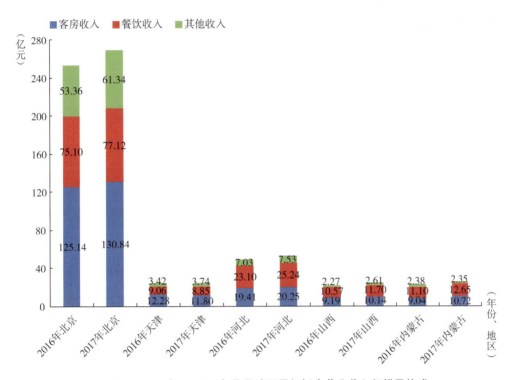

图 4-10　2016 年、2017 年华北地区星级饭店营业收入规模及构成

2017 年华北地区中，北京、天津、河北、山西和内蒙古营业收入分别为 269.30 亿元、24.39 亿元、53.02 亿元、24.44 亿元和 25.72 亿元，占比分别为 67.86%、6.15%、13.36%、6.16% 和 6.48%，其中北京占比最大。与 2016 年相比，北京、河北、山西和内蒙古营业收入同比增加，增幅分别为 6.19%、7.04%、10.98% 和 14.24%；天津营业收入同比下降，降幅为 1.52%。

2017 年华北地区星级饭店营业收入结构主要以客房和餐饮收入为主，占总收入的 80.46%。具体来看，与 2016 年表现一致，北京和天津星级饭店营业收入主要以客房收入为主，占总营业收入的比例分别为 48.59% 和 48.38%；河北、山西和内蒙古的营业收入主要以餐饮收入为主，占总营业收入的比例分别为 47.61%、47.86% 和 49.17%（表 4-1）。

表 4-1　2016 年、2017 年华北地区星级饭店营业收入比重构成

	客房收入占比（%）		餐饮收入占比（%）		其他收入占比（%）	
	2016 年	2017 年	2016 年	2017 年	2016 年	2017 年
华北地区	47.00	46.30	34.62	34.16	18.38	19.54
北　京	49.34	48.59	29.61	28.64	21.04	22.78
天　津	49.60	48.38	36.60	36.30	13.80	15.32
河　北	39.19	38.18	46.63	47.61	14.18	14.21
山　西	41.72	41.48	47.99	47.86	10.29	10.66
内蒙古	40.15	41.69	49.29	49.17	10.56	9.14

（2）百元固定资产实现营业收入

从星级饭店百元固定资产实现营业收入看，2017 年华北地区为 33.78 元，同比减少 1.75 元，降幅为 4.91%。具体来看，北京星级饭店固定资产投入创收能力最强，为 38.89 元，同比增加 0.49 元，增幅为 1.28%；天津为 19.41 元，同比减少 30.15 元，降幅为 60.84%；河北为 33.81 元，同比增加 2.33 元，增幅为 7.44%；山西为 26.21 元，同比增加 0.54 元，增幅为 2.10%；内蒙古为 24.09 元，同比增加 0.34 元，增幅为 1.43%（图 4-11）。

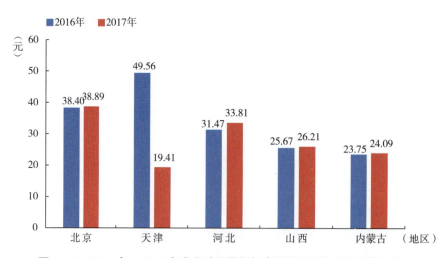

图 4-11　2016 年、2017 年华北地区星级饭店百元固定资产实现营业收入

（3）每间客房实现营业收入

从星级饭店每间客房实现营业收入看，2017年华北地区为13.91万元，同比减少3.34万元，降幅为19.38%。具体来看，北京为16.38万元，同比减少8.72万元，降幅为34.74%；天津为15.17万元，同比增加0.30万元，增幅为2.02%；河北为10.34万元，同比增加0.56万元，增幅为5.73%；山西为9.43万元，同比增加0.75万元，增幅为8.64%；内蒙古为9.33万元，同比减少0.84万元，降幅为8.26%（图4-12）。

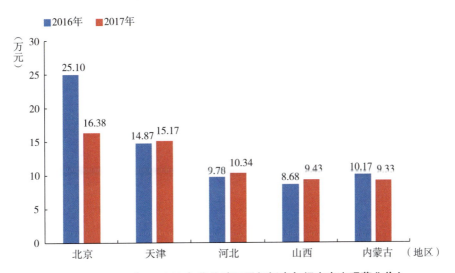

图4-12　2016年、2017年华北地区星级饭店每间客房实现营业收入

（4）百元营业收入占用固定资产

从星级饭店百元营业收入占用固定资产看，2017年华北地区为296.04元，同比增加14.54元，增幅为5.17%。具体来看，北京为257.11元，同比减少3.32元，降幅为1.27%；天津为515.16元，同比增加313.38元，增幅为155.31%；河北为295.81元，同比减少21.90元，降幅为6.89%；山西为381.48元，同比减少8.10元，降幅为2.08%；内蒙古为415.08元，同比减少6.00元，降幅为1.42%（图4-13）。

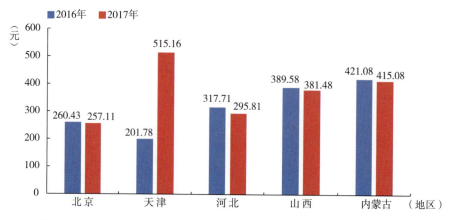

图 4-13　2016 年、2017 年华北地区星级饭店百元营业收入占用固定资产

3. 利润总额

从星级饭店利润总额看，2017 年华北地区全年盈利 2.43 亿元，同比减少 9.27 亿元，降幅为 79.24%。具体来看，只有北京近两年连续实现盈利，其他各地区均处于亏损状态。北京利润总额为 15.88 亿元，同比利润减少了 11.58 亿元，降幅为 42.17%；天津亏损 0.80 亿元，同比亏损减少 0.74 亿元，降幅为 48.05%；河北亏损 7.27 亿元，同比亏损增加 0.94 亿元，增幅为 14.85%；山西亏损 3.77 亿元，同比亏损减少 0.74 亿元，降幅为 16.41%；内蒙古亏损 1.62 亿元，同比亏损减少 1.77 亿元，降幅为 52.21%（图 4-14）。

图 4-14　2016 年、2017 年华北地区星级饭店利润总额

4. 人力资源情况

从星级饭店从业人数看，2017 年度华北地区为 18.79 万人，同比增加 0.5 万人，增幅为 2.75%。具体来看，北京为 8.76 万人，同比增加 0.26 万人，增幅为 3.06%；天津为 1.30 万人，同比减少 0.07 万人，降幅为 5.11%；河北为 4.27 万人，同比增加 0.03 万人，增幅为 0.71%；山西为 2.43 万人，同比减少 0.02 万人，降幅为 0.82%；内蒙古为 2.03 万人，同比增加 0.30 万人，增幅为 17.34%（图 4-15）。

图 4-15 2016 年、2017 年华北地区星级饭店从业人数及人房比

从星级饭店人房比看，2017 年度华北地区为 0.66 人 / 间，同比减少 0.19 人 / 间，降幅为 22.26%。具体来看，北京为 0.53 人 / 间，同比减少 0.31 人 / 间，降幅为 36.90%；天津为 0.81 人 / 间，同比减少 0.01 人 / 间，降幅为 1.22%；河北为 0.83 人 / 间，同比减少 0.01 人 / 间，降幅为 1.19%；山西为 0.94 人 / 间，同比减少 0.03 人 / 间，降幅为 3.09%；内蒙古为 0.74 人 / 间，同比减少 0.04 人 / 间，降幅为 5.13%。

三、东北地区行业分析（黑龙江、吉林和辽宁）

1. 数量分布

2017 年，东北地区星级饭店数量 638 家，以三星级、四星级饭店为主。具体来看，五星级饭店共计 35 家，占东北地区星级饭店总量的 5.49%；四星级饭店共计 149 家，占东北地区星级饭店总量的 23.35%；三星级饭店共计 338 家，占东北地区星级饭店总量的 52.98%；二星级饭店共计 114 家，占东北地区星级饭店总量的 17.87%；一星级饭店共计 2 家，占东北地区星级饭店总量的 0.31%（图 4-16）。

与 2016 年相比，东北地区五星级饭店占比同比增加 15.53%，四星级饭店占比同比增加 4.51%，三星级饭店占比同比减少 0.70%，二星级饭店占比同比减少 6.62%，一星级饭店占比同比减少 25.18%。

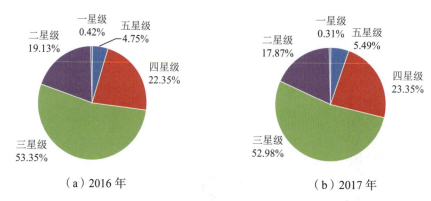

图 4-16　2016 年、2017 年东北地区星级饭店整体分布

从星级饭店数量分布来看，2017 年黑龙江星级饭店数量 187 家，占东北星级饭店数量的 29.31%；吉林星级饭店数量 115 家，占东北地区星级饭店数量的 18.03%；辽宁星级饭店数量 336 家，占东北地区星级饭店数量的 52.66%。

与 2016 年相比，黑龙江、吉林和辽宁星级饭店数量同比均呈现下降趋势，分别减少 11 家、54 家和 13 家，降幅分别为 5.56%、31.95% 和 3.72%（图 4-17）。

图 4-17　2016 年、2017 年东北地区各星级饭店分布情况

从星级饭店数量分布结构来看，2017年东北地区三星级饭店占主导地位，其次是四星级、二星级、五星级和一星级饭店。具体来看，黑龙江一星级至五星级饭店数量分别为1家、30家、103家、47家和6家，占黑龙江省饭店总量的比例分别为0.53%、16.04%、55.08%、25.13%和3.12%；吉林一星级至五星级饭店数量分别为0家、23家、57家、32家和3家，占吉林省饭店总量的比例分别为0%、20%、49.57%、27.83%和2.61%；辽宁一星级至五星级饭店数量分别为1家、61家、178家、70家和26家，占辽宁省饭店总量的比例分别为0.30%、18.15%、52.98%、20.83%和7.74%。

2. 营业收入分布

（1）营业收入及构成

2017年东北地区星级饭店实现营业收入81.30亿元，同比增加2.29%，其中实现客房收入37.75亿元，占东北地区星级饭店营业收入的46.43%；餐饮收入32.20亿元，占东北地区星级饭店营业收入的39.61%；其他收入11.35亿元，占东北地区星级饭店营业收入的13.96%（图4-18）。

图4-18　2016年、2017年东北地区星级饭店营业收入规模及构成

2017年东北地区中，黑龙江、吉林和辽宁营业收入分别为16.05亿元、14.45亿元和50.80亿元，占比分别为19.74%、17.77%和62.49%，其中辽宁占比最大。与2016年相比，黑龙江和吉林营业收入同比下降，降幅分别为13.21%和6.07%；辽宁营业收入同比增加，增幅为11.40%。

表 4-2　2016 年、2017 年东北地区星级饭店营业收入比重构成

	客房收入占比（%）		餐饮收入占比（%）		其他收入占比（%）	
	2016 年	2017 年	2016 年	2017 年	2016 年	2017 年
东北地区	47.07	46.43	40.84	39.61	12.10	13.96
黑龙江	51.26	52.18	34.30	32.45	14.43	15.37
吉　林	45.90	44.90	46.05	44.67	8.05	10.43
辽　宁	45.76	45.04	41.73	40.43	12.51	14.52

　　2017 年东北地区星级饭店营业收入结构主要以客房和餐饮收入为主，占总收入的比例为 86.04%。具体来看，与 2016 年表现一致，黑龙江和辽宁星级饭店客房收入超过餐饮收入，占总营业收入的比例分别为 52.18% 和 45.04%；吉林星级饭店客房和餐饮收入相当，占总营业收入的比例分别为 44.90% 和 44.67%（表 4-2）。

　　（2）百元固定资产实现营业收入

　　从星级饭店百元固定资产实现营业收入看，2017 年东北地区为 29.39 元，同比增加 2.32 元，增幅为 8.58%。具体来看，辽宁星级饭店固定资产投入创收能力最强，为 31.07 元，同比增加 5.28 元，增幅为 20.47%；黑龙江为 27.07 元，同比减少 3.88 元，降幅为 12.54%；吉林为 26.85 元，同比减少 0.13 元，降幅为 0.48%（图 4-19）。

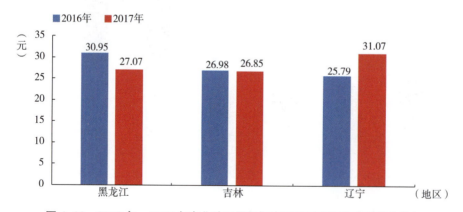

图 4-19　2016 年、2017 年东北地区星级饭店百元固定资产实现营业收入

　　（3）每间客房实现营业收入

　　从星级饭店每间客房实现营业收入看，2017 年东北地区为 9.50 万元，同比增加

0.4 万元，增幅为 4.34%。具体来看，黑龙江为 7.75 万元，同比减少 0.87 万元，降幅为 10.09%；吉林为 11.08 万元，同比增加 1.28 万元，增幅为 13.06%；辽宁为 9.80 万元，同比增加 0.71 万元，增幅为 7.81%（图 4–20）。

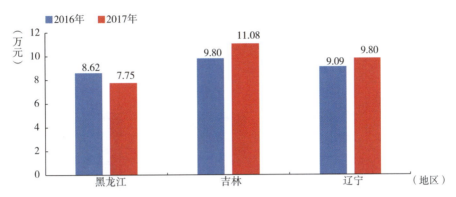

图 4–20　2016 年、2017 年东北地区星级饭店每间客房实现营业收入

（4）百元营业收入占用固定资产

从星级饭店百元营业收入占用固定资产看，2017 年东北地区为 340.21 元，同比减少 29.20 元，降幅为 7.90%。具体来看，黑龙江为 369.41 元，同比增加 46.35 元，增幅为 14.35%；吉林为 372.50 元，同比增加 1.91 元，增幅为 0.52%；辽宁为 321.81 元，同比减少 66.00 元，降幅为 17.02%（图 4–21）。

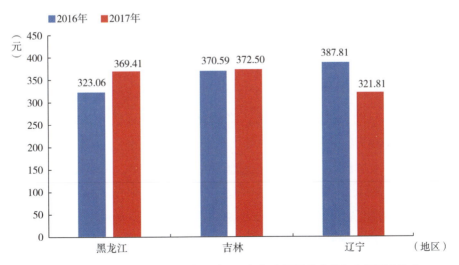

图 4–21　2016 年、2017 年东北地区星级饭店百元营业收入占用固定资产

3. 利润总额

从星级饭店利润总额看，2017 年东北地区全年亏损 4.93 亿元，同比减少 5.37 亿元，降幅为 52.15%。具体来看，黑龙江、吉林和辽宁均处于亏损状态，其中黑龙江亏损 0.63 亿元，同比亏损增加 0.46 亿元，增幅为 270.59%；吉林亏损 1.61 亿元，同比亏损减少 0.28 亿元，降幅为 14.81%；辽宁亏损 2.69 亿元，同比亏损减少 5.56 亿元，降幅为 67.39%（图 4–22）。

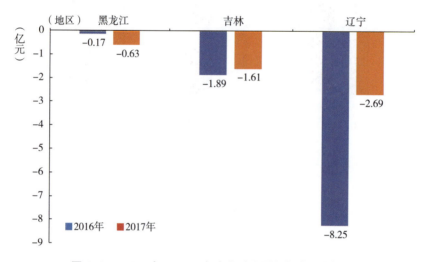

图 4–22　2016 年、2017 年东北地区星级饭店利润总额

4. 人力资源情况

从星级饭店从业人数看，2017 年东北地区为 5.58 万人，同比减少 0.51 万人，降幅为 8.33%。具体来看，黑龙江为 1.33 万人，同比增加 0.03 万人，增幅为 2.31%；吉林为 1.04 万人，同比减少 0.35 万人，降幅为 25.18%；辽宁为 3.21 万人，同比减少 0.19 万人，降幅为 5.59%（图 4–23）。

从星级饭店人房比看，2017 年东北地区为 0.65 人／间，同比减少 0.05 人／间，降幅为 6.50%。具体来看，黑龙江为 0.64 人／间，同比增加 0.03 人／间，增幅为 4.92%；吉林为 0.80 人／间，同比减少 0.08 人／间，降幅为 9.09%；辽宁为 0.62 人／间，同比减少 0.06 人／间，降幅为 8.82%。

图 4-23 2016 年、2017 年东北地区星级饭店从业人数及人房比

四、华东地区行业分析（上海、江苏、浙江、安徽、福建和山东）

1. 数量分布

2017 年，华东地区星级饭店数量 2508 家，以三星级、四星级饭店为主。具体来看，五星级饭店共计 339 家，占华东地区星级饭店总量的 13.52%；四星级饭店共计 755 家，占华东地区星级饭店总量的 30.10%；三星级饭店共计 1143 家，占华东地区星级饭店总量的 45.57%；二星级饭店共计 263 家，占华东地区星级饭店总量的 10.49%；一星级饭店共计 8 家，占华东地区星级饭店总量的 0.32%（图 4-24）。

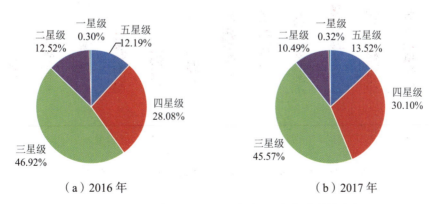

（a）2016 年 　　　　　　　　　（b）2017 年

图 4-24 2016 年、2017 年华东地区星级饭店整体分布

与 2016 年相比，华东地区五星级饭店占比同比增加 10.88%，四星级饭店占比同比增加 7.22%，三星级饭店占比同比减少 2.86%，二星级饭店占比同比减少 16.26%，一星级饭店占比同比增加 7.93%。

从星级饭店数量分布来看，2017 年上海星级饭店数量 223 家，占华东星级饭店数量的 8.89%；江苏星级饭店数量 514 家，占华东地区星级饭店数量的 20.49%；浙江星级饭店数量 585 家，占华东地区星级饭店数量的 23.33%；安徽星级饭店数量 294 家，占华东地区星级饭店数量的 11.72%；福建星级饭店数量 306 家，占华东地区星级饭店数量的 12.20%；山东星级饭店数量 586 家，占华东地区星级饭店数量的 23.37%。

与 2016 年相比，上海、江苏、浙江、安徽、福建和山东星级饭店数量同比分别减少 4 家、47 家、66 家、18 家、28 家和 36 家，降幅分别为 1.76%、8.38%、10.14%、5.77%、8.38% 和 5.79%（图 4-25）。

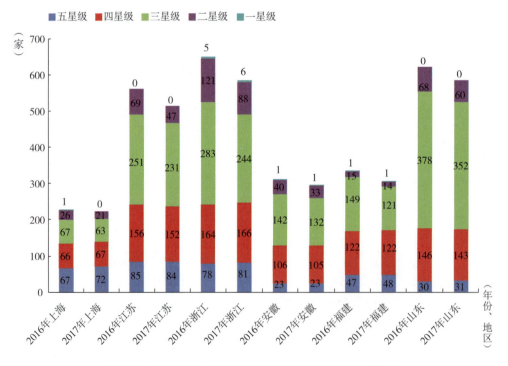

图 4-25　2016 年、2017 年华东地区各星级饭店分布情况

从星级饭店数量分布结构来看，2017年华东地区三星级饭店占主导地位，其次是四星级饭店、二星级饭店、五星级饭店和一星级饭店。具体来看，上海一星级至五星级饭店数量分别为0家、21家、63家、67家和72家，占上海市饭店总量的比例分别为0%、9.42%、28.25%、30.04%和32.29%；江苏一星级至五星级饭店数量分别为0家、47家、231家、152家和84家，占江苏省饭店总量的比例分别为0%、9.14%、44.94%、29.57%和16.34%；浙江一星级至五星级饭店数量分别为6家、88家、244家、166家和81家，占浙江省饭店总量的比例分别为1.03%、15.04%、41.71%、28.38%和13.85%；安徽一星级至五星级饭店数量分别为1家、33家、132家、105家和23家，占安徽省饭店总量的比例分别为0.34%、11.22%、44.90%、35.71%和7.82%；福建一星级至五星级饭店数量分别为1家、14家、121家、122家和48家，占福建省饭店总量的比例分别为0.33%、4.58%、39.54%、39.87%和15.69%；山东一星级至五星级饭店数量分别为0家、60家、352家、143家和31家，占山东省饭店总量的比例分别为0%、10.42%、60.07%、24.4%和5.29%。

2. 营业收入分布

（1）营业收入及构成

2017年华东地区星级饭店实现营业收入814.56亿元，同比增加1.92%，其中实现客房收入343亿元，占华东地区星级饭店营业收入的42.11%；餐饮收入362.87亿元，占华东地区星级饭店营业收入的44.55%；其他收入108.70亿元，占华东地区星级饭店营业收入的13.34%。

2017年华东地区中，上海、江苏、浙江、安徽、福建和山东营业收入分别为212.65亿元、163.40亿元、186.57亿元、51.16亿元、86亿元和114.78亿元，占比分别为26.11%、20.06%、22.90%、6.28%、10.56%和14.09%，其中上海占比最大。与2016年同期相比，上海、江苏、安徽和山东营业收入同比增加，增幅分别为6.32%、3.40%、3.43%和3.79%；浙江和福建营业收入同比下降，降幅为4.23%和0.33%（图4-26）。

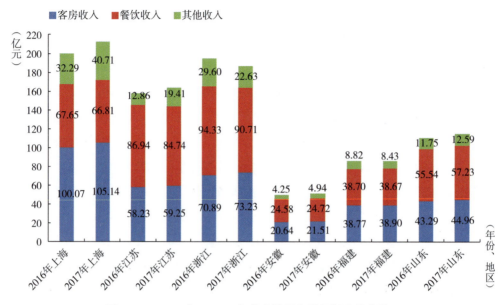

图 4-26　2016 年、2017 年华东地区各星级饭店分布情况

2017 年华东地区星级饭店营业收入结构主要以客房和餐饮收入为主，占总收入的比例为 86.66%。具体来看，与 2016 年表现一致，上海和福建星级饭店客房收入超过餐饮收入，占总营业收入的比例分别为 49.44% 和 45.24%；江苏、浙江、安徽和山东星级饭店餐饮收入超过客房收入，占总营业收入的比例分别为 51.86、48.62%、48.31% 和 49.86%（表 4-3）。

表 4-3　2016 年、2017 年华东地区星级饭店营业收入比重构成

	客房收入占比（%）		餐饮收入占比（%）		其他收入占比（%）	
	2016 年	2017 年	2016 年	2017 年	2016 年	2017 年
华东地区	41.53	42.11	46.01	44.55	12.46	13.34
上　海	50.03	49.44	33.83	31.42	16.14	19.14
江　苏	36.85	36.26	55.01	51.86	8.14	11.88
浙　江	36.39	39.25	48.42	48.62	15.19	12.13
安　徽	41.73	42.04	49.68	48.31	8.59	9.65
福　建	44.93	45.24	44.85	44.96	10.22	9.80
山　东	39.15	39.17	50.22	49.86	10.63	10.97

（2）百元固定资产实现营业收入

从星级饭店百元固定资产实现营业收入看，2017 年华东地区为 48.14 元，同比增加 0.93 元，增幅为 1.97%。具体来看，上海星级饭店固定资产投入创收能力最强，为 65.20 元，同比增加 4.77 元，增幅为 7.89%；江苏为 45.90 元，同比减少 0.21 元，降幅为 0.46%；浙江为 43.47 元，同比减少 1.54 元，降幅为 3.42%；安徽为 38.14 元，同比增加 1.31 元，增幅为 3.56%；福建为 57.99 元，同比减少 1.10 元，降幅为 1.86%；山东为 38.47 元，同比增加 3.36 元，增幅为 9.57%（图 4-27）。

图 4-27　2016 年、2017 年华东地区星级饭店百元固定资产实现营业收入

（3）每间客房实现营业收入

从星级饭店每间客房实现营业收入看，2017 年华东地区为 19.71 万元，同比增加 0.94 万元，增幅为 5.03%。具体来看，上海为 36.25 万元，同比增加 1.48 万元，增幅为 4.26%；江苏为 20.72 万元，同比增加 1.54 万元，增幅为 8.03%；浙江为 18.97 万元，同比减少 0.30 万元，降幅为 1.56%；安徽为 11.93 万元，同比增加 0.76 万元，增幅为 6.80%；福建为 16.43 万元，同比增加 0.44 万元，增幅为 2.75%；山东为 13.98 万元，同比增加 1.20 万元，增幅为 9.39%（图 4-28）。

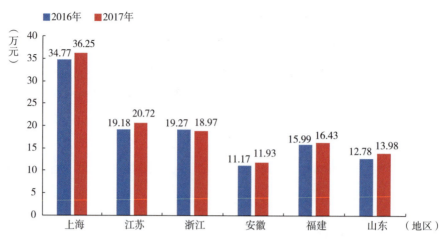

图 4-28　2016 年、2017 年华东地区星级饭店每间客房实现营业收入

（4）百元营业收入占用固定资产

从星级饭店百元营业收入占用固定资产看，2017 年华东地区为 207.74 元，同比减少 4.10 元，降幅为 1.93%。具体来看，上海为 153.37 元，同比减少 12.12 元，降幅为 7.32%；江苏为 217.87 元，同比增加 1.02 元，增幅为 0.47%；浙江为 230.06 元，同比增加 7.89 元，增幅为 3.55%；安徽为 262.20 元，同比减少 9.30 元，降幅为 3.43%；福建为 172.45 元，同比增加 3.20 元，增幅为 1.89%；山东为 259.96 元，同比减少 16.93 元，降幅为 6.11%（图 4-29）。

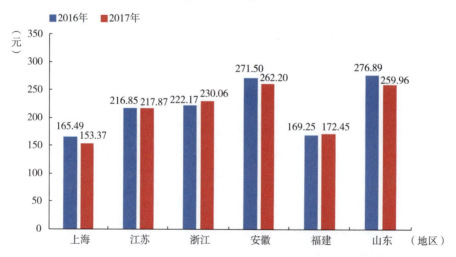

图 4-29　2016 年、2017 年华东地区星级饭店百元营业收入占用固定资产

3.利润总额

从星级饭店利润总额看，2017年华东地区全年盈利48.85亿元，同比增加27.65亿元，增幅为130.36%。具体来看，2017年只有山东亏损，其他各地区均实现盈利。上海利润总额为33.45亿元，同比利润增加3.96亿元，增幅为13.43%；江苏盈利5.29亿元，同比利润增加6.99亿元，增幅为411.18%；浙江盈利8.03亿元，同比利润增加10.78亿元，增幅为392%；安徽盈利0.90亿元，同比盈利增加1.22亿元，增幅为381.25%；福建盈利3.37亿元，同比利润增加1.50亿元，增幅为80.21%；山东亏损2.18亿元，同比利润增加3.21亿元，增幅为59.55%（图4-30）。

图4-30 2016年、2017年华东地区星级饭店利润总额

4.人力资源情况

从星级饭店从业人数看，2017年华东地区为36.71万人，同比减少2.84万人，降幅为7.17%。具体来看，上海为5.08万人，同比减少0.22万人，降幅为4.15%；江苏为7.45万人，同比减少0.55万人，降幅为6.88%；浙江为8.76万人，同比减少0.75万人，降幅为7.89%；安徽为3.31万人，同比减少0.14万人，降幅为4.06%；福建为4.85万人，同比减少0.50万人，降幅为9.35%；山东为7.27万人，同比减少0.67万人，降幅为8.44%（图4-31）。

图4-31　2016年、2017年华东地区星级饭店从业人数及人房比

从星级饭店人房比看，2017年华东地区为0.89人/间，同比减少0.04人/间，降幅为4.34%。具体来看，上海为0.87人/间，同比减少0.05人/间，降幅为5.43%；江苏为0.94人/间，同比减少0.03人/间，降幅为3.09%；浙江为0.89人/间，同比减少0.05人/间，降幅为5.32%；安徽为0.77人/间，同比减少0.01人/间，降幅为1.28%；福建为0.93人/间，同比减少0.06人/间，降幅为6.06%；山东为0.89人/间，同比减少0.03人/间，降幅为3.26%。

五、华南地区行业分析（广东、广西和海南）

1.数量分布

2017年度，华南地区星级饭店数量1148家，以三星级、四星级饭店为主。具体来看，五星级饭店共计136家，占华南地区星级饭店总量的11.85%；四星级饭店共计260家，占华南地区星级饭店总量的22.65%；三星级饭店共计622家，占华南地区星级饭店总量的54.18%；二星级饭店共计126家，占华南地区星级饭店总量的10.98%；一星级饭店共计4家，占华南地区星级饭店总量的0.35%（图4-32）。

与2016年相比，华南地区五星级饭店占比同比增加4.13%，四星级饭店占比同比增加6.62%，三星级饭店占比同比减少0.72%，二星级饭店占比同比减少11.56%，一星级饭店占比同比减少12.40%。

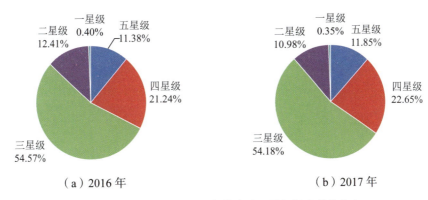

（a）2016 年 （b）2017 年

图 4-32 2016 年、2017 年华南地区星级饭店整体分布

从星级饭店数量分布来看，2017 年度广东星级饭店数量 658 家，占华南星级饭店数量的 57.32%；广西星级饭店数量 370 家，占华南地区星级饭店数量的 32.23%；海南星级饭店数量 120 家，占华南地区星级饭店数量的 10.45%。

与 2016 年相比，广东、广西和海南星级饭店数量同比分别减少 65 家、40 家和 4 家，降幅分别为 8.99%、9.76% 和 3.23%（图 4-33）。

图 4-33 2016 年、2017 年华南地区各星级饭店分布情况

从星级饭店数量分布结构来看，2017 年华南地区三星级饭店占主导地位，其次是四星级、五星级、二星级和一星级饭店。具体来看，广东一星级至五星级饭店数量

分别为 2 家、53 家、363 家、137 家和 103 家，占广东省饭店总量的比例分别为 0.30%、8.05%、55.17%、20.82% 和 15.65%；广西一星级至五星级饭店数量分别为 0 家、68 家、208 家、85 家和 9 家，占广西省饭店总量的比例分别为 0%、18.38%、56.22%、22.97% 和 2.43%；海南一星级至五星级饭店数量分别为 2 家、5 家、51 家、38 家和 24 家，占海南省饭店总量的比例分别为 1.67%、4.17%、42.50%、31.67% 和 20%。

2. 营业收入分布

（1）营业收入及构成

2017 年华南地区星级饭店实现营业收入 294.01 亿元，同比减少 0.22%，其中实现客房收入 140.89 亿元，占华南地区星级饭店营业收入的 47.92%；餐饮收入 111.10 亿元，占华南地区星级饭店营业收入的 37.79%；其他收入 42.02 亿元，占华南地区星级饭店营业收入的 14.29%。

2017 年华南地区中，广东、广西和海南营业收入分别为 210.83 亿元、37.76 亿元和 45.42 亿元，占比分别为 71.71%、12.84% 和 15.45%，其中广东省占比最大。与 2016 年相比，广东和广西营业收入同比下降，降幅分别为 0.17% 和 4.46%；海南营业收入同比增加，增幅为 3.39%（图 4-34）。

图 4-34　2016 年、2017 年华南地区星级饭店营业收入规模及构成

2017 年华南地区星级饭店营业收入结构主要以客房和餐饮收入为主，占总收入的比例为 85.71%。具体来看，与 2016 年表现一致，广西和海南星级饭店客房和餐饮收入差距较大，均以客房收入为主，客房占总营业收入的比例分别为 49.32% 和 59.02%；广东星级饭店客房和餐饮收入相当，占总营业收入的比例分别为 45.28% 和 40.35%（表 4-4）。

表 4-4　2016 年、2017 年华南地区星级饭店营业收入比重构成

	客房收入占比（％）		餐饮收入占比（％）		其他收入占比（％）	
	2016 年	2017 年	2016 年	2017 年	2016 年	2017 年
华南地区	47.08	47.92	38.90	37.79	14.02	14.29
广　东	44.04	45.28	41.47	40.35	14.49	14.37
广　西	49.19	49.32	38.96	37.25	11.85	13.43
海　南	59.79	59.02	26.51	26.32	13.70	14.66

（2）百元固定资产实现营业收入

从星级饭店百元固定资产实现营业收入看，2017 年华南地区为 45.83 元，同比增加 7.88 元，增幅为 20.76%。具体来看，广东星级饭店固定资产投入创收能力最强，为 48.90 元，同比增加 11.54 元，增幅为 30.89%；广西为 42.05 元，同比增加 1.71 元，增幅为 4.24%；海南为 37.67 元，同比减少 1.20 元，降幅为 3.09%（图 4-35）。

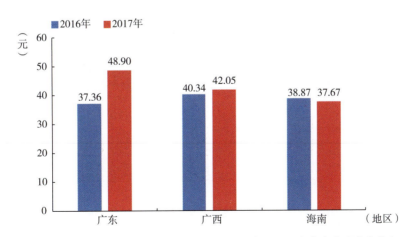

图 4-35　2016 年、2017 年华南地区星级饭店百元固定资产实现营业收入

（3）每间客房实现营业收入

从星级饭店每间客房实现营业收入看，2017年华南地区为15.46万元，同比增加0.80万元，增幅为5.47%。具体来看，广东为18.16万元，同比增加0.77万元，增幅为4.43%；广西为7.79万元，同比增加0.28万元，增幅为3.73%；海南为17.77万元，同比增加1.44万元，增幅为8.82%（图4-36）。

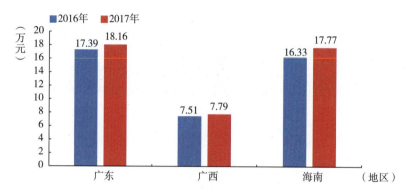

图4-36　2016年、2017年华南地区星级饭店每间客房实现营业收入

（4）百元营业收入占用固定资产

从星级饭店百元营业收入占用固定资产看，2017年华南地区为218.19元，同比减少45.29元，降幅为17.19%。具体来看，广东为204.49元，同比减少63.19元，降幅为23.61%；广西为237.82元，同比减少10.09元，降幅为4.07%；海南为265.49元，同比增加8.25元，增幅为3.21%（图4-37）。

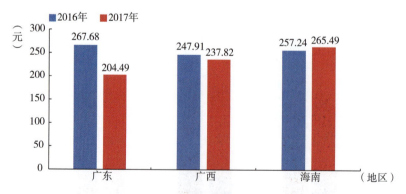

图4-37　2016年、2017年华南地区星级饭店百元营业收入占用固定资产

3. 利润总额

从星级饭店利润总额看，2017 年华南地区全年盈利 25.07 亿元，同比增加 5.26 亿元，增幅为 26.55%。具体来看，广东和海南实现盈利，广西处于亏损状态。广东利润总额为 22.41 亿元，同比利润增加 9.81 亿元，增幅为 77.86%；广西亏损 0.79 亿元，同比亏损增加 3.85 亿元，增幅为 125.82%；海南利润总额为 3.46 亿元，同比利润减少 0.70 亿元，降幅为 16.83%（图 4-38）。

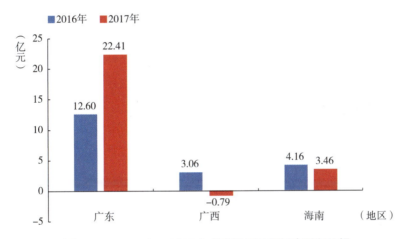

图 4-38　2016 年、2017 年华南地区星级饭店利润总额

4. 人力资源情况

从星级饭店从业人数看，2017 年华南地区为 15.51 万人，同比减少 2.13 万人，降幅为 12.10%。具体来看，广东为 10.42 万人，同比减少 1.87 万人，降幅为 15.22%；广西为 3.03 万人，同比减少 0.23 万人，降幅为 7.06%；海南为 2.06 万人，同比减少 0.04 万人，降幅为 1.90%（图 4-39）。

从星级饭店人房比看，2017 年华南地区为 0.82 人 / 间，同比减少 0.06 人 / 间，降幅为 7.09%。具体来看，广东为 0.90 人 / 间，同比减少 0.11 人 / 间，降幅为 10.89%；广西为 0.62 人 / 间，与 2016 年持平；海南为 0.81 人 / 间，同比增加 0.03 人 / 间，增幅为 3.85%。

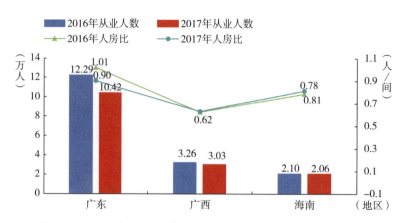

图 4-39 2016 年、2017 年华南地区星级饭店从业人数及人房比

六、华中地区行业分析（江西、河南、湖北和湖南）

1.数量分布

2017 年度，华中地区星级饭店数量 1400 家，以三星级、四星级饭店为主。具体来看，五星级饭店共计 74 家，占华中地区星级饭店总量的 5.29%；四星级饭店共计 335 家，占华中地区星级饭店总量的 23.93%；三星级饭店共计 741 家，占华中地区星级饭店总量的 52.93%；二星级饭店共计 245 家，占华中地区星级饭店总量的 17.50%；一星级饭店共计 5 家，占华中地区星级饭店总量的 0.36%（图 4-40）。

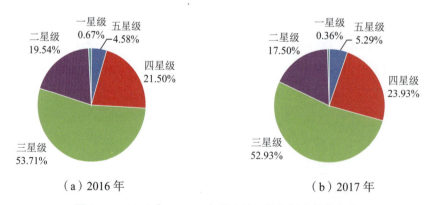

（a）2016 年   （b）2017 年

图 4-40 2016 年、2017 年华中地区星级饭店整体分布

与 2016 年相比，华中地区五星级饭店占比同比增加 15.35%，四星级饭店占

比同比增加 11.32%，三星级饭店占比同比减少 1.45%，二星级饭店占比同比减少 10.45%，一星级饭店占比同比减少 47%。

从星级饭店数量分布来看，2017 年度江西星级饭店数量 281 家，占华中星级饭店数量的 20.07%；河南星级饭店数量 389 家，占华中地区星级饭店数量的 27.79%；湖北星级饭店数量 364 家，占华中地区星级饭店数量的 26%；湖南星级饭店数量 366 家，占华中地区星级饭店数量的 26.14%。

与 2016 年相比，江西、河南和湖南星级饭店数量同比分别减少 9 家、22 家和 53 家，降幅分别为 3.10%、5.35% 和 12.65%；湖北星级饭店数量保持不变（图 4-41）。

图 4-41　2016 年、2017 年华中地区各星级饭店分布情况

从星级饭店数量分布结构来看，2017 年华中地区三星级饭店占主导地位，其次是四星级饭店、二星级饭店、五星级饭店和一星级饭店。具体来看，江西一星级至五星级饭店数量分别为 0 家、19 家、149 家、100 家和 13 家，占江西省饭店总量的比例分别为 0%、6.76%、53.02%、35.59% 和 4.63%；河南一星级至五星级饭店数量分别为 1 家、55 家、231 家、83 家和 19 家，占河南省饭店总量的比例分别为 0.26%、14.14%、59.38%、21.34% 和 4.88%；湖北一星级至五星级饭店数量分别为 4 家、86 家、166 家、85 家和 23 家，占湖北省饭店总量的比例分别为 1.10%、23.63%、45.60%、23.35% 和 6.32%；湖南一星级至五星级饭店数量分别为 0 家、85 家、195 家、67 家和 19 家，占湖南省饭店总量的比例分别为 0%、23.22%、53.28%、18.31% 和 5.19%。

2. 营业收入分布

（1）营业收入及构成

2017 年华中地区星级饭店实现营业收入 203.18 亿元，同比增加 1.28%，其中实现客房收入 93.17 亿元，占华中地区星级饭店营业收入的 45.85%；餐饮收入 87.98 亿元，占华中地区星级饭店营业收入的 43.30%；其他收入 22.03 亿元，占华中地区星级饭店营业收入的 10.84%。

2017 年华中地区中，江西、河南、湖北和湖南营业收入分别为 33.02 亿元、57.66 亿元、52.13 亿元和 60.36 亿元，占比分别为 16.25%、28.38%、25.66% 和 29.71%，其中湖南占比最大。与 2016 年相比，江西省和湖南省营业收入同比下降，降幅分别为 3.15% 和 4.27%；河南省和湖北省营业收入同比增加，增幅分别为 2.62% 和 10.28%（图 4-42）。

图 4-42　2016 年、2017 年华中地区星级饭店营业收入规模及构成

2017 年华中地区星级饭店营业收入结构主要以客房和餐饮收入为主，占总收入的比例为 89.15%。具体来看，与 2016 年表现一致，江西省星级饭店客房收入超过餐饮收入，占总营业收入的比例分别为 49.49% 和 40.80%；河南省星级饭店餐饮收入超过客房收入，占总营业收入的比例分别为 47.87% 和 40.76%；湖北省星级饭店客房收入和餐饮收入差距较大，占总营业收入的比例分别为 51.48% 和 39.37%；湖南省星级饭店客房和餐饮收入相当，占总营业收入的比例分别为 43.87% 和 43.71%（表 4-5）。

表 4-5　2016 年、2017 年华中地区星级饭店营业收入比重构成

	客房收入占比（%）		餐饮收入占比（%）		其他收入占比（%）	
	2016 年	2017 年	2016 年	2017 年	2016 年	2017 年
华中地区	44.07	45.85	43.32	43.30	12.61	10.84
江　西	46.74	49.49	41.53	40.80	11.73	9.71
河　南	39.25	40.76	46.22	47.87	14.53	11.37
湖　北	49.16	51.48	40.10	39.37	10.73	9.15
湖　南	43.10	43.87	44.11	43.71	12.79	12.42

（2）百元固定资产实现营业收入

从星级饭店百元固定资产实现营业收入看，2017 年华中地区为 42.09 元，同比增加 1.64 元，增幅为 4.06%。具体来看，江西星级饭店固定资产投入创收能力最强，为 45.58 元，同比增加 2.95 元，增幅为 6.92%；河南为 43.43 元，同比增加 1.55 元，增幅为 3.70%；湖北为 41.62 元，同比增加 3.13 元，增幅为 8.13%；湖南为 39.65 元，和 2016 年持平（图 4-43）。

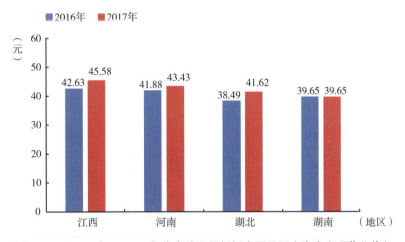

图 4-43　2016 年、2017 年华中地区星级饭店百元固定资产实现营业收入

（3）每间客房实现营业收入

从星级饭店每间客房实现营业收入看，2017 年华中地区为 10.71 万元，同比增加 0.36 万元，增幅为 3.48%。具体来看，江西为 8.51 万元，同比减少 0.10 万元，

降幅为 1.16%；河南为 10.95 万元，同比增加 0.53 万元，增幅为 5.09%；湖北为 10.73 万元，同比增加 0.74 万元，增幅为 7.41%；湖南为 12.16 万元，同比增加 0.25 万元，增幅为 2.10%（图 4-44）。

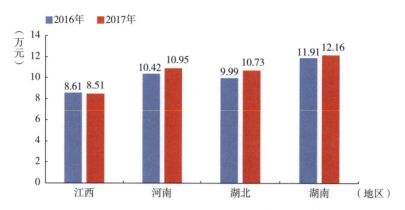

图 4-44 2016 年、2017 年华中地区星级饭店每间客房实现营业收入

（4）百元营业收入占用固定资产

从星级饭店百元营业收入占用固定资产看，2017 年华中地区为 237.59 元，同比减少 9.64 元，降幅为 3.90%。具体来看，江西为 219.41 元，同比减少 15.15 元，降幅为 6.46%；河南为 230.26 元，同比减少 8.53 元，降幅为 3.57%；湖北为 240.29 元，同比减少 19.49 元，降幅为 7.50%；湖南为 252.20 元，同比减少 0.01 元，降幅为 0.004%（图 4-45）。

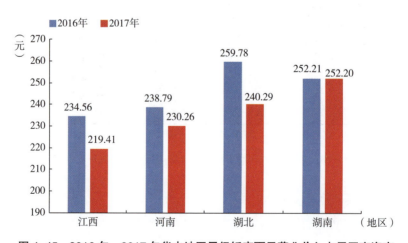

图 4-45 2016 年、2017 年华中地区星级饭店百元营业收入占用固定资产

3. 利润总额

从星级饭店利润总额看，2017年华中地区全年盈利3.46亿元，同比增加29.46亿元，增幅为113.31%。具体来看，江西、湖北和湖南实现盈利，河南处于亏损状态。江西利润总额为0.91亿元，同比利润增加0.32亿元，增幅为54.24%；河南亏损1.95亿元，同比亏损减少7.15亿元，降幅为78.57%；湖北利润总额为0.74亿元，同比利润增加17.57亿元，增幅为104.40%；湖南利润总额为3.76亿元，同比增加4.42亿元，增幅为669.70%（图4-46）。

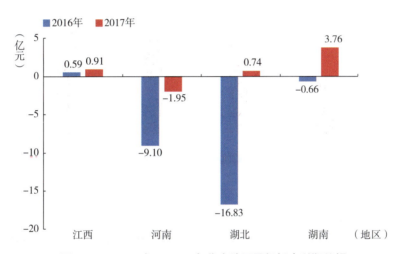

图4-46 2016年、2017年华中地区星级饭店利润总额

4. 人力资源情况

从星级饭店从业人数看，2017年华中地区为14.48万人，同比减少0.79万人，降幅为5.17%。具体来看，江西为2.48万人，同比减少0.15万人，降幅为5.70%；河南为4.22万人，同比减少0.35万人，降幅为7.66%；湖北为3.63万人，同比增加0.17万人，增幅为4.91%；湖南为4.14万人，同比减少0.48万人，降幅为10.39%（图4-47）。

从星级饭店人房比看，2017年华中地区为0.76人/间，同比减少0.02人/间，降幅为3.11%。具体来看，江西为0.64人/间，同比减少0.03人/间，降幅为4.48%；河南为0.80人/间，同比减少0.05人/间，降幅为5.88%；湖北为0.75人/间，同比增加 0.02 人 / 间，增幅为 2.74%；湖南为 0.84 人 / 间，同比减少 0.03 人 / 间，降幅为 3.45%。

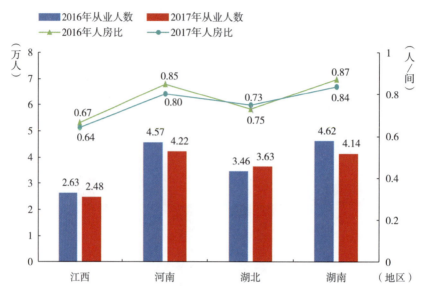

图 4-47　2016 年、2017 年华中地区星级饭店从业人数及人房比

七、西南地区行业分析（重庆、四川、贵州、云南和西藏）

1. 数量分布

2017 年，西南地区星级饭店数量 1331 家，以三星级、四星级饭店为主。具体来看，五星级饭店共计 80 家，占西南地区星级饭店总量的 6.01%；四星级饭店共计 313 家，占西南地区星级饭店总量的 23.52%；三星级饭店共计 533 家，占西南地区星级饭店总量的 40.05%；二星级饭店共计 377 家，占西南地区星级饭店总量的 28.32%；一星级饭店共计 28 家，占西南地区星级饭店总量的 2.10%（图 4-48）。

与 2016 年相比，西南地区五星级饭店占比同比增加 12.74%，四星级饭店占比同比增加 15.75%，三星级饭店占比同比减少 1.80%，二星级饭店占比同比减少 7.93%，一星级饭店占比同比减少 25.13%。

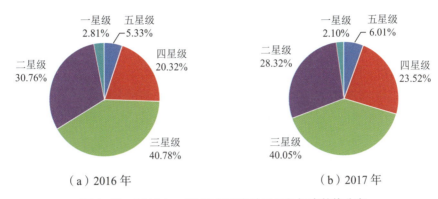

（a）2016 年　　　　　　　　　　　（b）2017 年

图 4-48　2016 年、2017 年西南地区星级饭店整体分布

从星级饭店数量分布来看，2017 年重庆星级饭店数量 188 家，占西南星级饭店数量的 14.12%；四川星级饭店数量 323 家，占西南地区星级饭店数量的 24.27%；贵州星级饭店数量 232 家，占西南地区星级饭店数量的 17.43%；云南星级饭店数量 518 家，占西南地区星级饭店数量的 38.92%；西藏星级饭店数量 70 家，占西南地区星级饭店数量的 5.26%。

与 2016 年相比，重庆、贵州和云南星级饭店数量同比分别减少 9 家、34 家和 41 家，降幅分别为 4.57%、12.78% 和 7.33%；四川和西藏星级饭店数量同比分别增加 25 家和 2 家，增幅分别为 8.39% 和 2.94%（图 4-49）。

图 4-49　2016 年、2017 年西南地区各星级饭店分布情况

从星级饭店数量分布结构来看，2017 年西南地区三星级饭店占主导地位，其次是二星级饭店、四星级饭店、五星级饭店和一星级饭店。具体来看，重庆一星级至五星级饭店数量分别为 0 家、24 家、85 家、51 家和 28 家，占重庆市饭店总量的比例分别为 0%、12.77%、45.21%、27.13% 和 14.89%；四川一星级至五星级饭店数量分别为 2 家、77 家、121 家、98 家和 25 家，占四川省饭店总量的比例分别为 0.62%、23.84%、37.46%、30.34% 和 7.74%；贵州一星级至五星级饭店数量分别为 8 家、65 家、95 家、58 家和 6 家，占贵州省饭店总量的比例分别为 3.45%、28.02%、40.95%、25.00% 和 2.59%；云南一星级至五星级饭店数量分别为 17 家、195 家、212 家、75 家和 19 家，占云南省饭店总量的比例分别为 3.28%、37.64%、40.93%、14.48% 和 3.67%；西藏一星级至五星级饭店数量分别为 1 家、16 家、20 家、31 家和 2 家，占西藏自治区饭店总量的比例分别为 1.43%、22.86%、28.57%、44.29% 和 2.86%。

2. 营业收入分布

（1）营业收入及构成

2017 年西南地区星级饭店实现营业收入 175.25 亿元，同比增加 6.00%，其中实现客房收入 87.01 亿元，占西南地区星级饭店营业收入的 49.65%；餐饮收入 60.40 亿元，占西南地区星级饭店营业收入的 34.46%；其他收入 27.84 亿元，占西南地区星级饭店营业收入的 15.89%。

2017 年西南地区中，重庆、四川、贵州、云南和西藏营业收入分别为 37.35 亿元、61.96 亿元、26.16 亿元、39.19 亿元和 10.59 亿元，占比分别为 21.31%、35.36%、14.93%、22.36% 和 6.04%，其中四川占比最大。与 2016 年同期相比，四川、贵州、云南和西藏营业收入同比增加，增幅分别为 11.16%、1.99%、5.46% 和 89.81%；重庆营业收入同比下降，降幅为 9.33%（图 4-50）。

图 4-50　2016 年、2017 年西南地区星级饭店营业收入规模及构成

2017 年西南地区星级饭店营业收入结构主要以客房和餐饮收入为主，占总收入的比例为 84.11%。具体来看，与 2016 年表现一致，重庆、四川、贵州、云南和西藏星级饭店客房收入均超过餐饮收入，占总营业收入的比例分别为 46.92%、44.45%、56.60%、56.91% 和 45.66%（表 4-6）。

表 4-6　2016 年、2017 年西南地区星级饭店营业收入比重构成

	客房收入占比（%）		餐饮收入占比（%）		其他收入占比（%）	
	2016 年	2017 年	2016 年	2017 年	2016 年	2017 年
西南地区	50.50	49.65	34.06	34.46	15.43	15.89
重　庆	44.27	46.92	37.65	36.77	18.08	16.31
四　川	45.80	44.45	35.45	38.18	18.76	17.37
贵　州	57.40	56.60	32.61	32.80	9.99	10.61
云　南	57.89	56.91	30.70	29.61	11.42	13.47
西　藏	62.69	45.66	22.85	26.66	14.46	27.68

（2）百元固定资产实现营业收入

从星级饭店百元固定资产实现营业收入看，2017年西南地区为32.76元，同比增加0.40元，增幅为1.24%。具体来看，贵州星级饭店固定资产投入创收能力最强，为49.60元，同比增加8.10元，增幅为19.52%；重庆为41.46元，同比减少1.95元，降幅为4.49%；四川为35.44元，同比增加0.11元，增幅为0.31%；云南为23.05元，同比增加0.16元，增幅为0.70%；西藏为22.38元，同比增加6.05元，增幅为37.05%（图4-51）。

图4-51　2016年、2017年西南地区星级饭店百元固定资产实现营业收入

（3）每间客房实现营业收入

从星级饭店每间客房实现营业收入看，2017年西南地区为10.60万元，同比增加0.52万元，增幅为5.20%。具体来看，重庆为13.48万元，同比减少0.84万元，降幅为5.87%；四川为13.14万元，同比增加0.41万元，增幅为3.22%；贵州为9.81万元，同比增加0.66万元，增幅为7.21%；云南为7.08万元，同比增加0.52万元，增幅为7.93%；西藏为12.64万元，同比增加4.45万元，增幅为54.33%（图4-52）。

图 4-52　2016 年、2017 年西南地区星级饭店每间客房实现营业收入

（4）百元营业收入占用固定资产

从星级饭店百元营业收入占用固定资产看，2017 年西南地区为 305.28 元，同比减少 3.79 元，降幅为 1.23%。具体来看，重庆为 241.18 元，同比增加 10.82 元，增幅为 4.70%；四川为 282.17 元，同比减少 0.84 元，降幅为 0.30%；贵州为 201.61 元，同比减少 39.33 元，降幅为 16.32%；云南为 439.90 元，同比减少 3.03 元，降幅为 0.69%；西藏为 446.74 元，同比减少 165.61 元，降幅为 27.04%（图 4-53）。

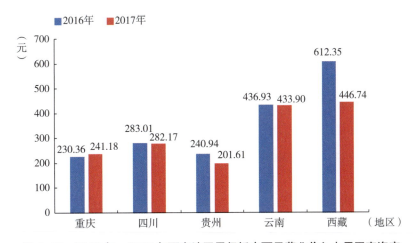

图 4-53　2016 年、2017 年西南地区星级饭店百元营业收入占用固定资产

3.利润总额

从星级饭店利润总额看，2017 年西南地区全年盈利 0.26 亿元，同比增加 2.80

亿元，增幅为 110.27%。具体来看，只有贵州近两年连续实现盈利，其他各地区均处于亏损状态。重庆亏损 0.22 亿元，同比亏损减少 0.44 亿元，降幅为 66.67%；四川亏损 0.54 亿元，同比亏损减少 2.46 亿元，降幅为 82%；贵州利润总额为 1.63 亿元，同比利润增加 0.65 亿元，增幅为 66.33%；云南亏损 0.26 亿元，同比亏损增加 0.42 亿元，增幅为 262.50%；西藏亏损 0.35 亿元，同比亏损增加 0.34 亿元，增幅为 3400%（图 4-54）。

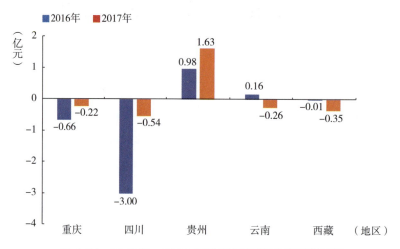

图 4-54　2016 年、2017 年西南地区星级饭店利润总额

4. 人力资源情况

从星级饭店从业人数看，2017 年西南地区为 12.60 万人，同比减少 0.62 万人，降幅为 4.70%。具体来看，重庆为 2.26 万人，同比减少 0.59 万人，降幅为 20.70%；四川为 4.04 万人，同比增加 0.26 万人，增幅为 6.88%；贵州为 1.69 万人，同比减少 0.18 万人，降幅为 9.63%；云南为 4.16 万人，同比减少 0.18 万人，降幅为 4.15%；西藏为 0.46 万人，同比增加 0.07 万人，增幅为 17.95%（图 4-55）。

从星级饭店人房比看，2017 年西南地区为 0.76 人 / 间，同比减少 0.04 人 / 间，降幅为 5.42%。具体来看，重庆为 0.81 人 / 间，同比减少 0.18 人 / 间，降幅为 18.18%；四川为 0.86 人 / 间，与 2016 年持平；贵州为 0.64 人 / 间，同比减少 0.03 人 / 间，降幅为 4.48%；云南为 0.75 人 / 间，同比减少 0.02 人 / 间，降幅为 2.60%；西藏为 0.54 人 / 间，同比减少 0.03 人 / 间，降幅为 5.26%。

图 4-55　2016 年、2017 年西南地区星级饭店从业人数及人房比

八、西北地区行业分析（陕西、甘肃、青海、宁夏和新疆）

1. 数量分布

2017 年，西北地区星级饭店数量 1182 家，以二星级至四星级饭店为主。具体来看，五星级饭店共计 31 家，占西北地区星级饭店总量的 2.62%；四星级饭店共计 233 家，占西北地区星级饭店总量的 19.71%；三星级饭店共计 671 家，占西北地区星级饭店总量的 56.77%；二星级饭店共计 242 家，占西北地区星级饭店总量的 20.47%；一星级饭店共计 5 家，占西北地区星级饭店总量的 0.42%（图 4-55）。

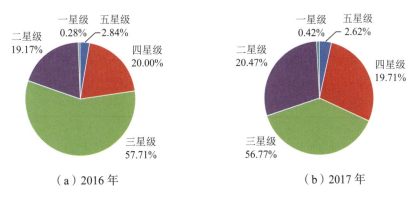

（a）2016 年　　　　　　　　（b）2017 年

图 4-56　2016 年、2017 年西北地区星级饭店整体分布

与 2016 年相比，西北地区五星级饭店占比同比减少 7.78%，四星级饭店占比同比减少 1.44%，三星级饭店占比同比减少 1.63%，二星级饭店占比同比增加 6.78%，一星级饭店占比同比增加 53.69%。

从星级饭店数量分布来看，2017 年陕西星级饭店数量 300 家，占西北星级饭店数量的 25.38%；甘肃星级饭店数量 304 家，占西北地区星级饭店数量的 25.72%；青海星级饭店数量 162 家，占西北地区星级饭店数量的 13.71%；宁夏星级饭店数量 94 家，占西北地区星级饭店数量的 7.95%；新疆星级饭店数量 322 家，占西北地区星级饭店数量的 27.24%。

与 2016 年相比，陕西、甘肃、青海和宁夏星级饭店数量同比分别增加 25 家、5 家、86 家和 4 家，增幅分别为 9.09%、1.67%、113.16% 和 4.44%；新疆星级饭店数量同比减少 28 家，降幅为 8.00%（图 4-57）。

图 4-57 2016 年、2017 年西北地区各星级饭店分布情况

从星级饭店数量分布结构来看，2017 年西北地区三星级饭店占主导地位，其次是二星级饭店、四星级饭店、五星级饭店和一星级饭店。具体来看，陕西一星级至五星级饭店数量分别为 0 家、60 家、180 家、45 家和 15 家，占陕西省饭店总量的比例分别为 0%、20%、60%、15% 和 5%；甘肃一星级至五星级饭店数量分别为 5 家、70 家、158 家、68 家和 3 家，占甘肃省饭店总量的比例分别为 1.64%、23.03%、

51.97%、22.37% 和 0.99%；青海一星级至五星级饭店数量分别为 0 家、57 家、68 家、36 家和 1 家，占青海省饭店总量的比例分别为 0%、35.19%、41.98%、22.22% 和 0.62%；宁夏一星级至五星级饭店数量分别为 0 家、4 家、57 家、33 家和 0 家，占宁夏回族自治区饭店总量的比例分别为 0%、4.26%、60.64%、35.11% 和 0%；新疆一星级至五星级饭店数量分别为 0 家、51 家、208 家、51 家和 12 家，占新疆维吾尔自治区饭店总量的比例分别为 0%、15.84%、64.60%、15.84% 和 3.73%。

2. 营业收入分布

（1）营业收入及构成

2017 年西北地区星级饭店实现营业收入 118.75 亿元，同比增加 2.75%，其中实现客房收入 56.47 亿元，占西北地区星级饭店营业收入的 47.56%；餐饮收入 50.21 亿元，占西北地区星级饭店营业收入的 42.28%；其他收入 12.07 亿元，占西北地区星级饭店营业收入的 10.16%。

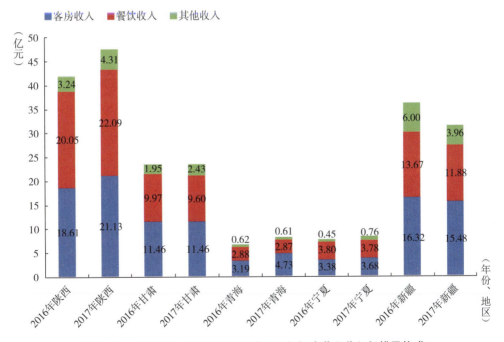

图 4-58　2016 年、2017 年西北地区星级饭店营业收入规模及构成

2017 年西北地区中，陕西、甘肃、青海、宁夏和新疆营业收入分别为 47.52 亿

元、23.48 亿元、8.20 亿元、8.22 亿元、31.32 亿元，占比分别为 40.02%、19.78%、6.90%、6.93% 和 26.37%，其中陕西占比最大。与 2016 年同期相比，陕西、甘肃、青海和宁夏营业收入同比增加，增幅分别为 13.41%、0.48%、22.58% 和 7.87%；新疆营业收入同比下降，降幅为 12.97%（图 4-58）。

2017 年西北地区星级饭店营业收入结构主要以客房和餐饮收入为主，占总收入的比例为 89.84%。具体来看，与 2016 年表现一致，陕西和宁夏星级饭店餐饮收入均超过客房收入，占总营业收入的比例分别为 46.48% 和 45.99%；甘肃、青海和新疆星级饭店客房收入均超过餐饮收入，占总营业收入的比例分别为 48.78%、57.65% 和 49.42%（表 4-7）。

表 4-7 2016 年、2017 年西北地区星级饭店营业收入比重构成

	客房收入占比（%）		餐饮收入占比（%）		其他收入占比（%）	
	2016 年	2017 年	2016 年	2017 年	2016 年	2017 年
西北地区	45.81	47.56	43.58	42.28	10.61	10.16
陕　西	44.42	44.46	47.85	46.48	7.73	9.07
甘　肃	49.02	48.78	42.65	40.86	8.33	10.35
青　海	47.62	57.65	43.07	34.96	9.30	7.39
宁　夏	44.28	44.80	49.79	45.99	5.93	9.21
新　疆	45.33	49.42	37.98	37.92	16.68	12.66

（2）百元固定资产实现营业收入

从星级饭店百元固定资产实现营业收入看，2017 年西北地区为 33.16 元，同比增加 0.71 元，增幅为 2.20%。具体来看，青海星级饭店固定资产投入创收能力最强，为 35.34 元，同比减少 2.94 元，降幅为 7.68%；陕西为 34.82 元，同比增加 2.20 元，增幅为 6.74%；甘肃为 34.29 元，同比增加 1.60 元，增幅为 4.89%；宁夏为 32.90 元，同比增加 1.60 元，增幅为 5.11%；新疆为 29.83 元，同比减少 1.62 元，降幅为 5.15%（图 4-59）。

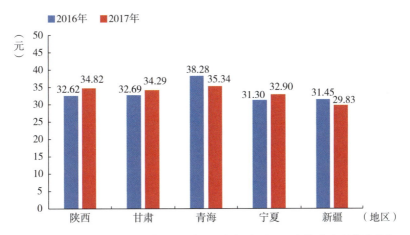

图4-59　2016年、2017年西北地区星级饭店百元固定资产实现营业收入

（3）每间客房实现营业收入

从星级饭店每间客房实现营业收入看，2017年西北地区为8.40万元，同比减少0.31万元，降幅为3.55%。具体来看，陕西为11.24万元，同比增加0.39万元，增幅为3.59%；甘肃为7.07万元，同比减少0.12万元，降幅为1.67%；青海为5.54万元，同比减少3.20万元，降幅为36.61%；宁夏为7.86万元，同比增加0.22万元，增幅为2.88%；新疆为7.69万元，同比减少0.48万元，降幅为5.88%（图4-60）。

图4-60　2016年、2017年西北地区星级饭店每间客房实现营业收入

（4）百元营业收入占用固定资产

从星级饭店百元营业收入占用固定资产看，2017年西北地区为301.61元，同

比减少 6.63 元，降幅为 2.15%。具体来看，陕西为 287.22 元，同比减少 19.38
元，降幅 6.32%；甘肃为 291.60 元，同比减少 14.32 元，降幅为 4.68%；青海
为 282.93 元，同比增加 21.73 元，增幅为 8.32%；宁夏为 303.91 元，同比减少
15.60 元，降幅为 4.88%；新疆为 335.21 元，同比增加 17.22 元，增幅为 5.42%
（图 4-61）。

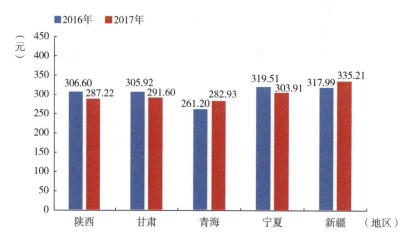

图 4-61　2016 年、2017 年西北地区星级饭店百元营业收入占用固定资产

3. 利润总额

从星级饭店利润总额看，2017 年西北地区全年亏损 2.68 亿元，同比亏损减少
6.48 亿元，降幅为 70.77%。具体来看，2017 年只有陕西实现微弱盈利，其他各地
区均处于亏损状态。陕西利润总额为 0.18 亿元，同比利润增加 2.19 亿元，增幅为
109.18%；甘肃亏损 1.26 亿元，同比亏损增加 1.93 亿元，增幅为 289.95%；青海亏
损 0.09 亿元，同比亏损增加 0.04 亿元，增幅为 87.43%；宁夏亏损 0.25 亿元，同比
亏损减少 5.76 亿元，降幅为 95.80%；新疆亏损 1.26 亿元，同比亏损减少 0.50 亿元，
降幅为 28.31%（图 4-62）。

图 4-62　2016 年、2017 年西北地区星级饭店利润总额

4. 人力资源情况

从星级饭店从业人数看，2017 年西北地区为 8.80 万人，同比减少 0.81 万人，降幅为 8.39%。具体来看，陕西为 2.99 万人，同比减少 0.46 万人，降幅为 13.33%；甘肃为 2.11 万人，同比减少 0.10 万人，降幅为 4.52%；青海为 0.75 万人，同比增加 0.17 万人，增幅为 29.31%；宁夏为 0.67 万人，同比减少 0.03 万人，降幅为 4.29%；新疆为 2.27 万人，同比减少 0.39 万人，降幅为 14.66%（图 4-63）。

图 4-63　2016 年、2017 年西北地区星级饭店从业人数及人房比

从星级饭店人房比看，2017 年西北地区为 0.62 人 / 间，同比减少 0.10 人 / 间，降幅为 14.01%。具体来看，陕西为 0.71 人 / 间，同比减少 0.18 人 / 间，降幅为 20.22%；甘肃为 0.64 人 / 间，同比减少 0.04 人 / 间，降幅为 5.88%；青海为 0.51 人 / 间，同比减少 0.25 人 / 间，降幅为 32.89%；宁夏为 0.64 人 / 间，同比减少 0.06 人 / 间，降幅为 8.57%；新疆为 0.56 人 / 间，同比减少 0.04 人 / 间，降幅为 6.67%。

Part II
Current Situation And Characteristics Analysis

The General Characteristics for the Development of China's Star-rated Hotels in 2017

The data of this report is derived from the statistical bulletin issued by the Ministry of Culture and Tourism. The first, second and fourth chapters adopt the statistical annual reports of national star-rated hotels, and the third chapter adopts the statistical quarterly reports of national star-rated hotels.

2017 Annual Statistical Report of National Star-rated Hotels shows that by the end of 2017, there were 10,645 star-rated hotels in China, of which 10,417 completed the filling of operating data in the national star-rated hotel statistical survey management system, and 9,566 star-rated hotels finally passed the review of provincial tourism authorities. According to these data, China's star-rated hotels showed the following characteristics in 2017.

I. Stable Changing of Star-rated Hotel Industry Scale

Based on the supply-side structural reform, the continuous enrichment of accommodation industry, the more rational industry investment and the structural adjustment of star-rated hotels themselves, the scale of star-rated hotel industry in 2017 was stable compared with 2016, which was shown in the following aspects: the number of star-rated hotels decreased by 295 year-on-year, with a decrease of 2.99%. The number of guestrooms was 1,470,600, an increase of 3.53% year-on-year. The number of beds was 2,505,500, with a year-on-year increase of 0.91%. Fixed assets amounted to 516.11 billion yuan, down by 0.26% year-on-year. Domestic hotels accounted for 96.08% of the investment entities, a decrease of 8% year-on-year.

In terms of the star-level structure, the number of four star-rated and five star-rated hotels is increasing, while the number of one to three star-rated hotels is decreasing. Specifically, the number of four star-rated and five star-rated hotels in 2017 was 2,412 and 816 respectively, with year-on-year growth of 2.07% and 2.00% respectively. The number of one to three star-rated hotels was 64, 1,660 and 4,614 respectively, with year-on-year decreases of 9.86%, 6.27% and 4.98% respectively.

The proportion of three star-rated hotels is the highest, the proportion of four star-rated and five star-rated hotels is increasing year by year, and the proportion of one star-rated and two star-rated hotels is decreasing year by year. Specifically, the proportion of three star-rated, four star-rated, two star-rated, five star-rated and one star-rated hotels in 2017 was 48.23%, 25.21%, 17.35%, 8.53% and 0.67%, respectively. The proportion of four star-rated and five star-rated hotels increased by 5.22% and 5.18%, and the proportion of one to three star-rated hotels decreased by 6.94%, 3.40% and 2.05%, respectively.

II. Significant Improvement in Overall Profitability

Based on the enhancement of customers' consumption ability, the effect of replacing operating tax with value-added tax, the progress of information technology and the improvement of star-rated hotels' own operation and management ability, the main operation indexes of star-rated hotels in 2017 showed a good trend of developing and improving of their profitability, compared with 2016. Of these, the total profit was 7.247 billion yuan, up by 1438.64% year-on-year. Operational revenue was 208.393 billion yuan, up by 2.80% year-on-year. The operational revenue of each hundred-yuan fixed assets was 40.38 yuan and the year-on-year growth was 3.06%. The revenue of each room is 141,700 yuan, a decrease of 0.70% year on year. The average occupancy rate was 54.80% and the year-on-year growth was 0.13%. The average guestroom price was 343.43 yuan per room night, with a year-on-year increase of 2.66%. The number of employees was 1,124,100, down by 6.06% year-on-year. The staff to room ratio of was 0.76 people per room, down by 9.26% year-on-year.

III. Different Performances of All Star-rated Hotels

In 2017, all star-rated hotels showed different characteristics and trends in the main operating indexes.

In terms of total profits, two star-rated to five star-rated hotels showed an increase while the one star-rated hotels declined. Specifically, profits of two star-rated to five star-rated hotels totaled 178 million yuan, 185 million yuan, 320 million yuan and 6.557 billion yuan, with year-on-year growth of 11.25%, 108.96%, 114.70% and 44.59%, respectively. The profit of one star-rated hotels totaled 0.07 million yuan, a drop of 58.82% year-on-year.

In terms of operational revenue, two, four star-rated and five star-rated hotels are growing, while one and three star-rated hotels are declining. Specifically, the operational revenue of two, four star-rated and five star-rated hotels was 7.855 billion yuan, 71.491 billion yuan and 81.271 billion yuan, respectively with year-on-year growth of 4.21%, 1.57% and 6.42%, respectively. The operational revenue of one star-rated and three star-rated hotels was 113 million yuan and 47.643 billion yuan, respectively, with a year-on-year decrease of 2.59% and 1.39%.

From operational revenue of each hundred-yuan fixed assets, one star-rated to three star-rated hotels showed a trend of increase while four star-rated and five star-rated hotel declined. Specifically, the operational revenue of each hundred-yuan fixed assets of one star-rated to three star-rated hotels was 73.40 yuan, 42.94 yuan and 46.76 yuan, with year-on-year growth of 53.11%, 58.33% and 2.36%, respectively. The operational revenue of each hundred-yuan fixed assets in four star-rated and five star-rated hotels was 37.05 yuan and 40.08 yuan, with year-on-year decrease of 4.51% and 6.14%, respectively.

In terms of operational revenue per room, the growth of one, two and five star-rated hotels showed a trend of increase while three and four star-rated hotels declined. Specifically, the operational revenue per room of one, two and five star-rated hotel is

37,200 yuan, 63,100 yuan and 283,800 yuan respectively, with year-on-year growth of 1.09%, 3.61% and 2.10%. The operational revenue per room of three star-rated and four star-rated hotels was 370,500 yuan and 141,900 yuan respectively, with year-on-year decrease of 4.51% and 5.21% respectively.

From the average occupancy rate, one, four star-rated and five star-rated hotels showed a trend of increase while two and three star-rated hotels declined. Specifically, the average occupancy rate of one, four star-rated and five star-rated hotels was 52.62%, 56.63% and 61.43%, respectively, with year-on-year growth of 0.84%, 1.82% and 4.88%. The average occupancy rate of two and three star-rated hotels was 47.08% and 51.30% respectively, with a year-on-year decrease of 10.10% and 2.32% respectively.

In terms of average daily rate, one star-rated to three star-rated hotels are increasing, while four star-rated and five star-rated hotels are decreasing. Specifically, the average room rate of one to three star-rated hotels was 102.39 yuan per room night, 171.17 yuan per room night and 220.36 yuan, with year-on-year growth of 1.99%, 9.96% and 5.11%, respectively. The average daily rate of four star-rated and five star-rated hotels was 328.06 yuan per room night and 612.35 yuan per room night, respectively, with a year-on-year decrease of 1.39% and 2.22%.

In terms of number of employees, one, three to five star-rated hotels showed a trend of decrease while two star-rated hotels increased. Specifically, the employees in one, three to five star-rated hotels were 1,200, 346,400, 417,700 and 297,200 respectively, with year-on-year decreases of 9.09%, 12.70%, 3.31% and 1.75% respectively. Two star-rated hotel employees numbered 61,600, up by 0.33% year-on-year.

From the perspective of staff to room ratio, two to five star-rated hotels showed a downward trend, while one star-rated hotels showed a trend of increase. Specifically, the staff to room ratio in two to five star-rated hotels was 0.49 people per room, 0.63 people per room, 0.83 people per room and 1.04 people per room, respectively with year-on-year decrease of 2.00%, 12.50%, 9.78% and 5.45%, respectively. The staff to room ratio of one star-rated hotel was 0.40 people per room, increased by 14.29% year-on-year.

IV. Steady Progress in Quarterly Development of Star-rated Hotels

From the first quarter to the fourth quarter of 2017, the star-rated hotels showed steady improvement in the main operating indexes.

From the perspective of operational revenue, the first quarter to the fourth quarter saw a steady rise from 47.621 billion yuan in operational revenue in the first quarter to 57.770 billion yuan in the fourth quarter, up by 10.149 billion yuan or 21.31%.

The revenue per available room climbed steadily from the first to the third quarter and recovered slightly in the fourth quarter. Specifically, the first to fourth quarters were 170.60 yuan per room night, 187.40 yuan per room night, 206.12 yuan per room night and 203.28 yuan per room night, with year-on-year growth rates of 4.04%, 3.86%, 7.63% and 5.29%, respectively.

The average occupancy rate is similar to the revenue performance rule of each available room for rent. From the first quarter to the third quarter, it climbed steadily and recovered slightly in the fourth quarter. Specifically, the average occupancy rate in the first to fourth quarters was 50.20%, 56.19%, 60.58 and 57.71%, respectively, with year-on-year growth of 2.57%, 1.61%, 3.50% and 1.96%.

From the perspective of average daily rate, the average daily rate in the first quarter to the fourth quarter was 339.87 yuan per room night, 333.50 yuan per room night, 340.25 yuan per room night and 352.23 yuan per room night, respectively, with year-on-year growth of 1.44%, 2.21%, 4.00% and 3.25%.

V. Imbalanced Regional Development of Star-rated Hotels

In 2017, from the main operating indexes, the regional markets of star-rated hotels saw an imbalanced development.

From the perspective of quantity distribution, east China has the largest number of

2,508 hotels, accounting for 26.22% of the total number of star-rated hotels in the country. The northeast China has the least distribution with 638 hotels, accounting for 6.67%. In the second place, it was central China, north China, southwest China, northwest China and south China, with a number of 1400, 1359, 1331, 1182 and 1148 hotels, accounting for 14.64%, 14.21%, 13.91%, 12.36% and 12.00% respectively.

In terms of total profits, east China had the most profit, with 4,885 million yuan. It was followed by south China, central China, north China and southwest China, with profits of 2,507 million yuan, 346 million yuan, 243 million yuan and 26 million yuan respectively. The northeast and northwest lost 493 million yuan and 268 million yuan, respectively.

From the perspective of operational revenue, east China has the highest revenue, with 81.456 billion yuan, accounting for 39.09% of the total revenue of star-rated hotels. The northeast China has the least revenue with 8.103 billion yuan, accounting for 3.90%. It was followed by north China, south China, central China, southwest China and northwest China, with operational revenue of 39.688 billion yuan, 29.401 billion yuan, 20.318 billion yuan, 17.525 billion yuan and 11.875 billion yuan, accounting for 19.04%, 14.11%, 9.75%, 8.41% and 5.70%, respectively.

In terms of the operational revenue of each hundred-yuan fixed assets, the east China has the most operational revenue with 48.14 yuan, while the northeast China has the least with 29.39 yuan. In the second places, there are south China, central China, north China, northwest and southwest China with 45.83 yuan, 42.09 yuan, 33.78 yuan, 33.16 yuan and 32.76 yuan of operational revenue of each hundred-yuan in fixed assets respectively.

In terms of operational revenue per room, east China has the most with 197,100 yuan. The northwest China has the lowest with 84,000 yuan. In the second places, there are south China, north China, central China, southwest China and northeast China. The operational revenue per room is 154,600 yuan, 139,100 yuan, 107,100 yuan, 106,000 yuan and 95,000 yuan respectively.

In terms of the number of employees, east China has the largest number of 367,100 employees. The least in the northeast was 55,800. It was followed by north China, south China, central China, southwest China and northwest China, with 187,900, 155,100,

144,800, 126,000 and 88,000 employees respectively.

In terms of the staff to room ratio, east China has the highest with 0.89 people per room. The least in the northwest region was 0.62 people per room. In the second place, there are south China, central China, southwest China, north China and northeast China, the staff to room ratio is 0.82 people per room, 0.76 people per room, 0.76 people per room, 0.66 people per room and 0.65 people per room, respectively.

Chapter II

The Scale and Operation of China's Star-rated Hotels

I. Scale and Composition

1. Industry Scale

(1) Number of Star-rated Hotels

From 2010 to 2017, except 2013, the number of star-rated hotels recovered, the overall number of star-rated hotels in China showed a downward trend, from 11,779 in 2010 to 9,566 in 2017, and the number of star-rated hotels decreased by 2,213 in total, down by 18.79% (Figure 2-1).

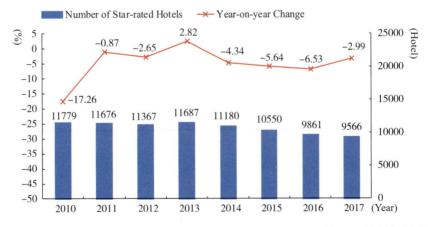

Figure 2-1　Number of Star-rated Hotels and its Year-on-year Change (2010~2017)

Compared with 2016, the number of star-rated hotels in 2017 decreased by 2.99% year-on-year.

(2) Number of Rooms

From 2010 to 2017, the number of star-rated hotel rooms in China fluctuated, from 1,476,400 rooms in 2010 to 1,470,600 rooms in 2017, and the number of rooms decreased 5,800 rooms, down by 0.39% Compared with the 18.79% decrease in the number of star-rated hotels in the above report, the change range of the number of rooms is smaller than that of hotels, reflecting a certain increase in the number of rooms in each star-rated hotels (Figure 2-2).

Compared with 2016, the number of star-rated hotel rooms increased by 3.53% year-on-year in 2017.

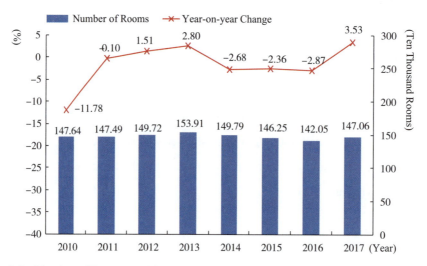

Figure 2-2   Number of Rooms and its Year-on-year Change of Star-rated Hotels (2010~2017)

(3) Number of Beds

From 2010 to 2017, the performance regularity of the number of beds and rooms in star-rated hotels in China was similar, showing a curve fluctuation. From 2,566,400 in 2010 to 2,505,500 in 2017, the number of rooms decreased by 60,900, with a decrease of 2.37% (Figure 2-3).

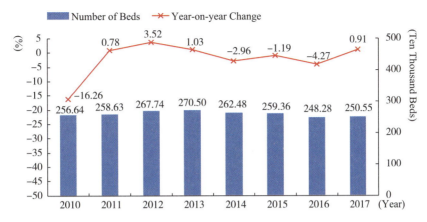

Figure 2-3   Number of Beds and its Year-on-year Change of Star-rated Hotels (2010~2017)

Compared with 2016, the number of star-rated hotel beds increased by 0.91% year-on-year in 2017.

(4) Fixed Assets Scale

From 2010 to 2015, the total fixed assets scale of star-rated hotels in China showed an overall growth trend, from 454.677 billion yuan in 2010 to 546.13 billion yuan in 2015, and the fixed assets scale increased by 91.453 billion yuan, an increase of 20.11%. From 2015 to 2017, the scale of fixed assets began to show a downward trend, with a year on year decrease of 5.25% in 2016 and 0.26% in 2017 (Figure 2-4).

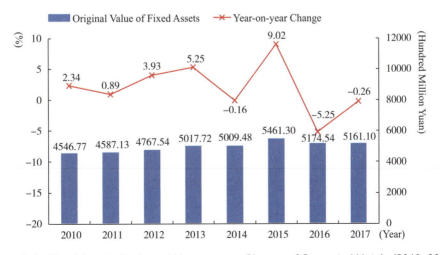

Figure 2-4   Fixed Assets Scale and Year-on-year Change of Star-rated Hotels (2010~2017)

2. Star-level structure

From 2010 to 2017, the number of four star-rated and five star-rated hotels showed an overall growth trend. From 2,002 in 2010 to 2,412 in 2017, the number of four star-rated hotels increased by 410, with an increase of 20.48%. The number of five star-rated hotels increased by 271 from 545 in 2010 to 816 in 2017, an increase of 49.72%. The overall number of one to three star-rated hotels is on a downward trend. From 212 in 2010 to 64 in 2017, the number of one star-rated hotels has decreased by 148, with a decrease of 69.81%. The number of two star-rated hotels decreased from 3,636 in 2010 to 1,660 in 2017, with a total decrease of 1,976, with a decrease of 54.35%. The number of three-star hotels dropped by 770 to 14.30% from 5,384 in 2010 to 4,614 in 2017 (Table 2-1).

Table 2-1　Composition and its Year-on-year Change of Number of Star-rated Hotels (2010~2017)

Year	Five star-rated hotels		Four star-rated hotels		Three star-rated hotels		Two star-rated hotels		One star-rated hotels	
	Quantity	Year-on-year Change	Quantity	Year-on-year Change	Quantity	Year-on-year Change	Quantity	Year-on-year Change	Quantity	Year-on-year Change
2010	545	7.71	2002	0.91	5384	-9.01	3636	-32.35	212	-53.41
2011	615	12.84	2148	7.29	5473	1.65	3276	-9.9	164	-22.64
2012	640	4.07	2186	1.77	5379	-1.72	3020	-7.81	142	-13.41
2013	739	15.47	2361	8.01	5631	4.68	2831	-6.26	125	-11.97
2014	745	0.81	2373	0.51	5406	-4	2557	-9.68	99	-20.8
2015	789	5.91	2375	0.08	5098	-5.7	2197	-14.03	91	-8.08
2016	800	1.39	2363	-0.51	4856	-4.75	1771	-19.39	71	-21.98
2017	816	2.00	2412	2.07	4614	-4.98	1660	-6.27	64	-9.86

According to the proportion of all star-rated hotels, from 2010 to 2017, the number of three star-rated hotels accounted for the highest proportion in the number of star-rated hotels in China, the proportion of one-star and two star-rated hotels declined year by year, and the proportion of four star-rated and five star-rated hotels increased year by year (Figure 2-5).

In 2017, the number of three star-rated hotel accounted for 48.23%, followed by four star-rated hotels accounted for 25.21%, two star-rated hotels accounted for 17.35%, five star-rated hotels accounted for 8.53% and one star-rated hotel accounted for 0.67%.

Figure 2-5   Proportion of Each Star-rated Hotel (2010~2017)

3. Pattern of Investment Entities

From the star-rated hotel major pattern of investment entities, between 2010 and 2017, domestic hotel always occupies the leading position in the investment entities, Hong Kong, Macao, Taiwan and foreign-invested hotels present a downward trend, the number of foreign investment hotels from 298, 274 in 2010 to 197, 178 in 2017 reduce 101 and 96 hotels, down by 33.89% and 35.04%, respectively (Figure. 2-6).

Figure 2-6 Pattern of Investment Entities and its Change of Star-rated Hotels (2010~2017)

II. Operational Revenues

1. Operational Revenue and its Composition

(1) Operational Revenue of Overall Star-rated Hotels

From 2010 to 2017, the operational revenue of star-rated hotels in China showed a curve fluctuation of first growth, then decline and then increase with the inflection point in 2012 and 2016, and the operational revenue decreased from 212.266 billion yuan in 2010 to 208.393 billion yuan in 2017, with a total decrease of 3.873 billion yuan and a decrease of 1.82%. Operational revenue was in a high growth period from 2010 to 2012, reaching a peak of 243.022 billion yuan in 2012. From 2013 to 2016, under the influence of policies, operational revenue began to decline, and in 2014, the decline was the largest, at 6.17%. Operational revenue increased by 5.667 billion yuan year-on-year in 2017, up by 2.80% (Figure 2-7).

Figure 2-7   Operational Revenue and its Year-on-year Change of Star-rated Hotels (2010~2017)

(2) Composition of Operational Revenue of Overall Star-rated Hotels

From 2010 to 2017, except 2012, the proportion of star-rated hotel rooms in the operational revenue was higher than that of food and beverage, especially after 2013, the proportion of rooms in the operational revenue increased year by year, and the proportion of food and beverage in the operational revenue decreased year by year (Figure 2-8).

In 2017, the proportion of star-rated hotel rooms in the operational revenue was 45.20%, and the proportion of food and beverage was 40.32%. Compared with 2016, the proportion of rooms in the operational revenue increased by 0.92%, and the decrease of food and beverage was 2.37%.

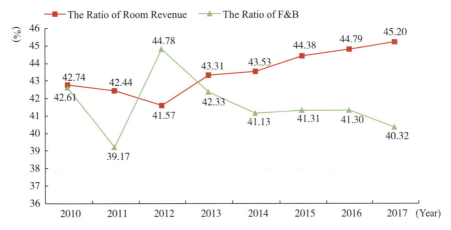

Figure 2-8   Composition of Operational Revenue and its Changes of Star-rated Hotels (2010~2017)

107

(3) Operational Revenue and its Composition of All Star-rated Hotels

From 2010 to 2017, the operational revenue of five star-rated hotels in China fluctuated slightly, but the overall growth trend was still on the rise, from 62.712 billion yuan in 2010 to 81.271 billion yuan in 2017, a total increase of 18.559 billion yuan, an increase of 29.59%. The proportion of rooms in operational revenue is higher than that of food and beverage in operationd revenue (Figure 2-9).

Figure 2-9   Operational Revenue and its Composition Changes of Five Star-rated Hotels (2010~2017)

From 2010 to 2017, the operational revenue of four star-rated hotels in China showed a curve fluctuation of growth first, then decrease and then increase after inflection point in 2012 and 2016, respectively. The proportion of rooms in the operational revenue was lower than that of food and beverage in operational revenue before 2013 and higher than that of food and beverage in operational revenue after 2013 (Figure 2-10).

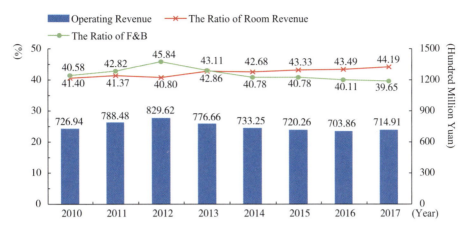

Figure 2-10   Operational Revenue and its Composition Changes of Four Star-rated

Hotels (2010~2017)

From 2010 to 2017, the operational revenue of three star-rated hotels in China showed a trend of first increase and then decrease with 2012 as the inflection point. Except for 2017, the proportion of rooms in operational revenue is lower than that of food and beverage in operational revenue (Figure 2-11).

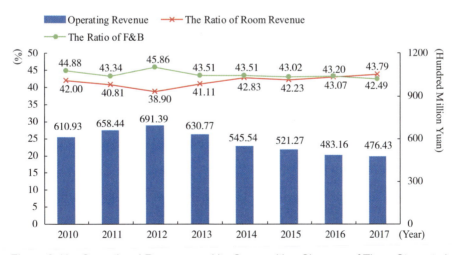

Figure 2-11   Operational Revenue and its Composition Changes of Three Star-rated

Hotels (2010~2017)

From 2010 to 2017, the operational revenue of two star-rated hotels in China was on the whole declining, from 15.399 billion yuan in 2010 to 7.855 billion yuan in 2017, a total of 7.544 billion yuan, a decrease of 48.99%. The proportion of rooms in operational revenue is higher than that of food and beverage in operational revenue (Figure 2-12).

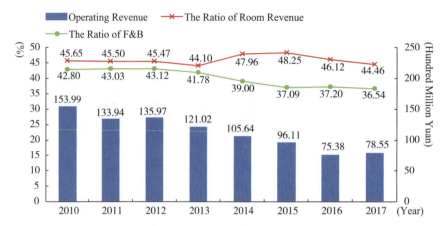

Figure 2-12   Operational Revenue and its Composition Changes of Two Star-rated Hotels (2010~2017)

From 2010 to 2017, the operational revenue of one star-rated hotels in China showed a downward trend on the whole, from 368 million yuan in 2010 to 113 million yuan in 2017, a total decrease of 255 million yuan, a decrease of 69.29%. Except for 2017, the proportion of rooms in operational revenue is higher than that of food and beverage in operational revenue (Figure 2-13).

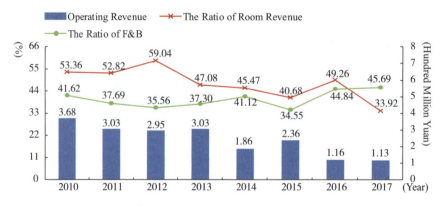

Figure 2-13   Operational Revenue and its Composition Changes of One Star-rated Hotels (2010~2017)

2. Operational Revenues of Each Hundred-yuan Fixed Assets

(1) Operational Revenues of Each Hundred-yuan Fixed Assets of Overall Star-rated Hotels

From 2010 to 2017, the operational revenue of each hundred-yuan fixed assets of star-rated hotels in China showed a curve fluctuation of first growth, then reduction and then growth at the inflection point of 2012 and 2015, among which, the increase was the largest in 2011, with a year-on-year increase of 3.78 yuan and an increase of 8.10%. In 2013, the decrease was the largest, with a year-on-year decrease of 5.27 yuan and a decrease of 10.34% (because there was no statistical information of each hundred-yuan fixed assets to achieve operational revenue in the statistical bulletin of national star-rated hotels in 2009, the year-on-year data in figure 2-14 was missing in 2010).

In 2017, the operational revenue of each hundred-yuan fixed assets of national star-rated hotels was 40.38 yuan, 1.2 yuan higher than that of 2016, with an increase of 3.06% (Figure 2-14).

Figure 2-14   Operational Revenues of Each Hundred-yuan Fixed Assets and its Year-on-year Change of Star-rated Hotels (2010~2017)

(2) Operational Revenues of Each Hundred-yuan Fixed Assets of Each Star-rated Hotels

From 2010 to 2017, the operational revenue of each hundred yuan the fixed assets

111

in four star-rated hotels and five star-rated hotels showed a continuous downward trend in 2011 and 2012 respectively. Among them, four star-rated and five star-rated hotels saw the biggest decrease in 2013, with a year-on-year decrease of 6.83 yuan and 3.33 yuan, respectively, and a decrease of 13.33% and 7.60% (Figure 2-15).

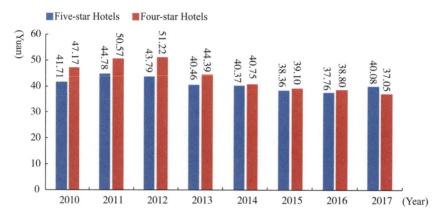

Figure 2-15   Operational Revenues of Each Hundred-yuan Fixed Assets and its Year-on-year Change of High Star-rated Hotels (2010~2017)

In 2017, the operational revenue of each hundred-yuan fixed assets in four star-rated and five star-rated hotels was 37.05 yuan and 40.08 yuan, respectively. Compared with 2016, the year-on-year decrease was 1.75 yuan and 2.32 yuan, and the decrease was 4.51% and 6.14%, respectively.

From 2010 to 2017, the operational revenue of each hundred-yuan fixed assets of one to three star-rated hotels showed a curve fluctuation. Among them, one star-rated hotels saw the largest increase in 2015, with a year-on-year increase of 49.29 yuan and an increase of 127.04%. The decrease of two star-rated hotels was the largest in 2016, with a decrease of 20.31 yuan and a decrease of 42.60% year-on-year. Three star-rated hotels saw the biggest decrease in 2015, with a year-on-year decrease of 11.76 yuan and a decrease of 24.19%. (Figure 2-16).

Figure 2-16   Operational Revenues of Each Hundred-yuan Fixed Assets and its Year-on-year

Change of Low Star-rated Hotels (2010~2017)

In 2017, the operational revenue of each hundred-yuan fixed assets of one to three star-rated hotels was 73.40 yuan, 42.94 yuan and 46.76 yuan, respectively. Compared with 2016, the year-on-year increase was 25.46 yuan, 15.82 yuan and 1.08 yuan, respectively, with the increase of 53.11%, 58.33% and 2.36%.

3. Operational Revenues per Room

(1) Operational Revenues per Room of Overall Star-rated Hotels

From 2010 to 2017, each room of star-rated hotels in China showed a curve fluctuation in operational revenue. Among them, 2011 saw the largest increase, with an year-on-year increase of 132,00 yuan, representing an increase of 9.18%. In 2013, the loss was the largest, with a year-on-year decrease of 13,300 thousand yuan, and the decrease was 8.19% (due to the lack of statistical information on each room's operational revenue index in the 2009 national star-rated hotel statistical bulletin, the data of 2010 in figure 2-17 were missing).

In 2017, the operational revenue per room of the national star-rated hotel was 141,700 yuan, which was reduced by 1000 yuan and 0.70% compared with that of 2016 (Figure 2-17).

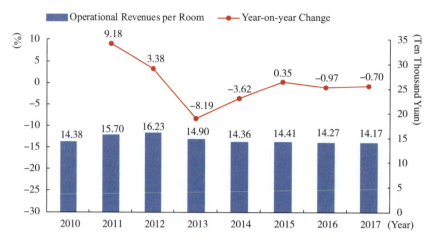

Figure 2-17   Operational Revenues per Room and its Year-on-year Change of Star-rated

Hotels (2010~2017)

(2) Operational Revenues per Room of Each Star-rated Hotels

From 2010 to 2017, the operational revenue per room of four star-rated hotels continued to decline after 2012. The revenue of each room in the five star-rated hotel fluctuates. Among them, four star-rated hotels saw the biggest decrease in 2013, with a year-on-year decrease of 219,00 yuan and a decrease of 11.54%. In 2012, the decrease of five star-rated hotels was the largest, with a year-on-year decrease of 30,400 yuan and a decrease of 9.05% (Figure 2-18).

Figure 2-18   Operational Revenues per Room and its Year-on-year Change of High Star-rated

Hotels (2010~2017)

In 2017, the operational revenue per room of four star-rated hotels was 141,900 yuan, 7,800 yuan lower than that of 2016, with a decrease of 5.21%. The revenue of each room in five star-rated hotels was 283,800 yuan, up by 5,600 yuan and up by 2.01% year-on-year.

From 2010 to 2017, the operational revenue per room of one and two star-rated hotels fluctuated in a curve. After 2012, the three star-rated hotel continued to decline. Among them, one star-rated hotels saw the largest increase in 2015, with a year-on-year increase of 16,300 yuan and an increase of 43.01%. Two star-rated hotels saw the largest increase in 2012, with a year-on-year increase of 6,300 yuan and an increase of 10.08%. In 2013, the loss of three star-rated hotels was the largest, with a decrease of 13,000 yuan and a decrease of 11.34% (Figure 2-19).

In 2017, the operational revenue of each hundred-yuan fixed assets in one star-rated and two star-rated hotels was 372,00 yuan and 63,100 yuan, respectively. Compared with 2016, the year-on-year increase was 400 yuan and 2,200 yuan, with the increase rate of 1.09% and 3.61% respectively. The operational revenue of each hundred-yuan fixed assets of three star-rated hotels was 86,200 yuan, a decrease of 1,800 yuan and a decrease of 2.05% year on year.

Figure 2-19   Operational Revenues per Room and its Year-on-year Change of Low Star-rated Hotels (2010~2017)

III. Total Profits

1. Total Profits of Overall Star-rated Hotels

From 2010 to 2017, the total profits of star-rated hotels in China fluctuated in a curve, among which, the total profits of star-rated hotels from 2013 to 2015 were shown as a loss, while the profits in other years were shown as a profit (because there was no statistical information about the total profits in the statistical bulletin of the star-rated hotels in 2009, the year-on-year data in figure 2-20 was missing).

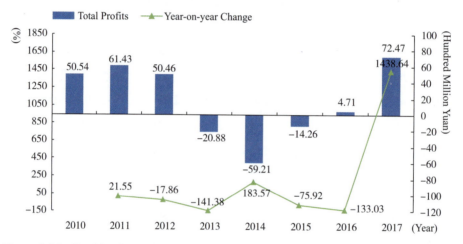

Figure 2-20   Total Profits and its Year-on-year Change of Star-rated Hotels (2010~2017)

As the government has replaced operational tax with value-added tax since May 1, 2016, the total profit of star-rated hotels in China turned into profit in 2016, and achieved a large increase in 2017, increasing by 6.776 billion yuan year-on-year, with an increase of 1438.64% (Figure 2-20).

2. Total Profits of Each Star-rated Hotel

From 2010 to 2017, five star-rated hotels were profitable. The total profits of four star-rated hotels fluctuated in a curve, among which losses were shown between 2013 and 2016 (Figure 2-21).

In 2017, the profits of four star-rated and five star-rated hotels totaled 320 million yuan and 6.557 billion yuan, respectively, increasing by 2.497 billion yuan and 2.022 billion yuan year-on-year compared with 2016, with an increase of 114.70% and 44.59%, respectively.

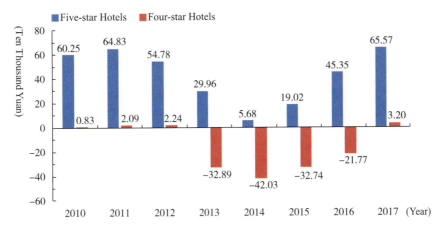

Figure 2-21   Total Profits and its Year-on-year Change of High Star-rated Hotels (2010~2017)

From 2010 to 2017, both one star-rated and two star-rated hotels were profitable. The three star-rated hotel did not turn a profit until 2017 (Figure 2-22).

Figure 2-22   Total Profits and its Year-on-year Change of Low Star-rated Hotels (2010~2017)

In 2017, the total profit of two star-rated and three star-rated hotels was 178 million yuan and 185 million yuan, respectively. Compared with 2016, the year-on-year increase was 18 million yuan and 2,249 million yuan, respectively, the increase was 11.25% and

108.96%. The profit of one star-rated hotels totaled 7 million yuan, a decrease of 10 million yuan and a decrease of 58.82% year-on-year.

IV. Average Occupancy Rate (AOR)

1. Average Occupancy Rate of Overall Star-rated Hotels

From 2010 to 2017, the average occupancy rate of star-rated hotels in China showed a curve fluctuation of first increase, then decrease and then increase at the inflection point of 2011 and 2015 respectively. Among them, the largest decrease in 2013 was 5.87% year-on-year. The largest increase in 2010 was 4.15% year-on-year (figure 2-23).

Figure 2-23   Average Occupancy Rate and its Year-on-year Change of Star-rated Hotels (2010~2017)

The average occupancy rate of national star-rated hotels was 54.80% in 2017, with a year-on-year increase of 0.13% compared with 2016.

2. Average Occupancy Rate of Each Star-rated Hotel

From 2010 to 2017, the average occupancy rate of four star-rated and five star-rated hotels showed a curve of increase first, then decrease and then increase at the inflection point in 2011 and 2015, respectively. Among them, four star-rated and five star-rated hotels saw the biggest decrease in 2013, with the year-on-year decrease of 5.64% and 6.43% respectively (Figure 2-24).

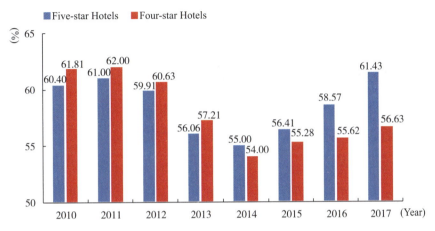

Figure 2-24   Average Occupancy Rate and its Year-on-year Change of High Star-rated

Hotels (2010~2017)

The average occupancy rates of four star-rated and five star-rated hotels were 56.63% and 61.43%, respectively, in 2017, with year-on-year increases of 1.82% and 4.88% compared with 2016.

From 2010 to 2017, the average occupancy rate of one-star and two star-rated hotels fluctuated. The three star-rated hotel is in a state of continuous decline (Figure 2-25).

Figure 2-25   Average Occupancy Rate and its Year-on-year Change of Low Star-rated

Hotels (2010~2017)

In 2017, the average occupancy rate of two star-rated and three star-rated hotels was 47.08% and 51.30%, respectively. Compared with 2016, the year-on-year decrease rate was 10.10% and 2.32%, respectively. The average occupancy rate of one star-rated hotels was 52.62% and the year-on-year increase was 0.84%.

V. Average Daily Rate (ADR)

1. Average Daily Rate of Overall Star-rated Hotels

From 2010 to 2017, except 2016, the average daily rate of star-rated hotels in China showed an overall growth trend. Among them, in 2011, the growth rate was the largest, 18.12 yuan per room night, and the year-on-year growth rate was 6.14% (because there was no statistical information of average daily rate index in the statistical bulletin of national star-rated hotels in 2009, the data of 2010 in figure 2-26 was missing).

Figure 2-26   Average Daily Rate and its Year-on-year Change of Star-rated Hotels (2010~2017)

In 2017, the average daily rate of star-rated hotels in China was 343.43 yuan per room night, which increased by 8.89 yuan per room night compared with 2016, with an increase of 2.66% year-on-year (Figure 2-26).

2. Average Daily Rate of Each Star-rated Hotel

Between 2010 and 2017, the average daily rate of four-star and five star-rated hotels continued to decline after 2012. Among them, the four star-rated hotels experienced the biggest decrease in 2015, which was 14.88 yuan per room night, and the year-on-year decrease was 4.19%. Five star-rated hotels saw the biggest decrease in 2016, which was 29.39 yuan per room night, and the year-on-year decrease was 4.48% (Figure 2-27).

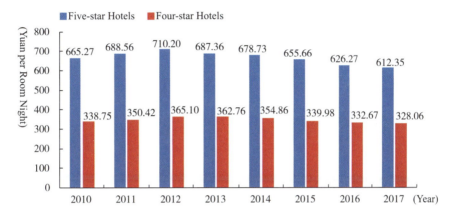

Figure 2-27　Average Daily Rate and its Year-on-year Change of High Star-rated
Hotels (2010~2017)

In 2017, the average daily rate of four star-rated hotels was 328.06 yuan per room night, which was 4.61 yuan per room night in decrease compared with 2016, with a year-on-year decrease of 1.39%. The average daily rate of five star-rated hotels was 612.35 yuan per room night, down 13.92 yuan per room night, with a year-on-year decrease of 2.22%.

From 2010 to 2017, the average daily rate of one star-rated to three star-rated hotels fluctuated in a curve. Among them, one star-rated hotels saw the biggest decrease in the number in 2016, with a year-on-year decrease of 32.37 yuan per room night, with a decrease of 24.38%. Two star-rated and three star-rated hotels showed the largest increase in 2017, with 15.50 yuan per room night and 10.71 yuan per room night , 9.96% and 5.11% increases year-on-year, respectively (Figure 2-28).

In 2017, the average daily rate of a one star-rated hotel was 102.39 yuan per room night, up by 2.00 yuan per room night compared with 2016, an increase of 1.99% year-on-year.

Figure 2-28   Average Daily Rate and its Year-on-year Change of Low Star-rated Hotel (2010~2017)

VI. Human Resources

1. Hotel Employees

(1) Hotel Employees of Overall Star-rated Hotels

From 2010 to 2017, except 2012, the number of employees in star-rated hotels in China was on the decline. In 2016, the decrease was the largest, with a year-on-year decrease of 147,900 people and a decrease of 11.00% (Figure 2-29).

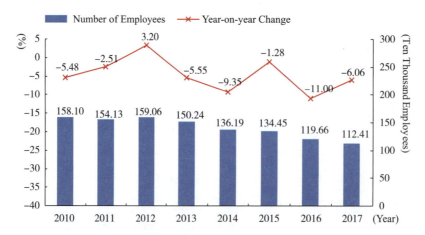

Figure 2-29   Hotel Employees and its Year-on-year Change of Star-rated Hotels (2010~2017)

In 2017, there were 1,124,100 employees in star-rated hotels nationwide, a year-on-year decrease of 72,500 and a decrease of 6.06% compared with 2016.

(2) Hotel Employees of Each Star-rated Hotels

From 2010 to 2017, the number of employees in four star-rated hotels and five star-rated hotels continued to decline after 2012 and 2013 respectively. Among them, four star-rated and five star-rated hotels saw the biggest decrease year-on-year in 2014, with a decrease of 55,000 and 21,500, respectively, and a decrease of 10.50% and 6.45% (Figure 2-30).

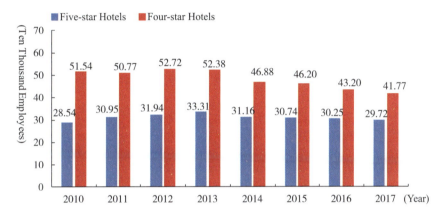

Figure 2-30   Hotel Employees and its Year-on-year Change of High Star-rated Hotels (2010~2017)

In 2017, 417,700 people were employed in four star-rated hotels, a year-on-year decrease of 14,300, a decrease of 3.31% compared with 2016. The number of people working in five star-rated hotels was 297,200, a year-on-year decrease of 5,300 and a decrease of 1.75%.

From 2010 to 2017, the number of employees in one to three star-rated hotels showed a downward trend. Among them, the number of one star-rated hotel employees decreased from 5,000 in 2010 to 1,200 in 2017, a decrease of 3,800 and 76.00%. The number of two star-rated hotel employees fell from 176,200 in 2010 to 61,600 in 2017, a decrease of 114,600 and 65.04%. The number of three star-rated hotel employees decreased from 599,000 in 2010 to 346,400 in 2017, a decrease of 252,600 and 42.17% (Figure 2-31).

Compared with 2016, the year-on-year increases in the number of one star-rated hotel and two star-rated hotel employees in 2017 were 9.09% and 0.33%, respectively three star-rated hotel employees decreased by 12.70% year-on-year.

Figure 2-31   Hotel Employees and its Year-on-year Change of Low Star-rated Hotels (2010~2017).

2. Staff to Room Ratio

(1) Staff to Room Ratio of Overall Star-rated Hotels

From 2010 to 2017, the ratio of national star-rated hotel staff to room declined as a whole, from 1.07 people per room in 2010 to 0.76 people per room in 2017, a total decrease of 0.31 people per room, with a decrease of 28.97%. In 2017, the decrease was the largest, with a year-on-year decrease of 0.08 people per room and a decrease of 9.26% (Figure 2-32).

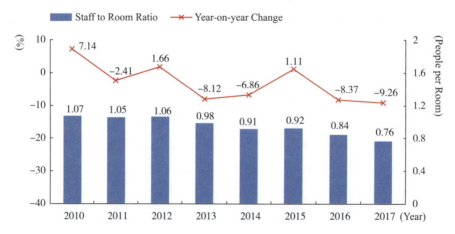

Figure 2-32   Staff to Room Ratio and its Year-on-year Change of Star-rated Hotels (2010~2017)

(2) Staff to Room Ratio of Each Star-rated Hotel

From 2010 to 2017, the ratio of four star-rated and five star-rated hotels showed a downward trend. Among them, the ratio of four star-rated hotel decreased by 0.44 people per room from 1.27 people per room in 2010 to 0.83 people per room in 2017, with a decrease of 34.65%. The ratio of five star-rated hotels decreased by 0.39 people per room from 1.43 people per room in 2010 to 1.04 people per room in 2017, with a decrease of 27.27% (Figure 2-33).

Compared with 2016, the year-on-year decrease of the four star-rated and five star-rated hotel rooms in 2017 was 9.78% and 5.45%, respectively.

Figure 2-33   Staff to Room Ratio and its Year-on-year Change of High Star-rated Hotels (2010~2017)

From 2010 to 2017, the ratio of one to three-star hotels also showed a downward trend. Among them, the one star-rated hotel room ratio decreased by 0.10 people per room from 0.50 people per room in 2010 to 0.40 people per room in 2017, with a decrease of 20.00%. The ratio of two star-rated hotel decreased by 0.22 people per room from 0.71 people per room in 2010 to 0.49 people per room in 2017, a decrease of 30.99%. The ratio of three star-rated hotel decreased by 0.35 people per room from 0.98 people per room in 2010 to 0.63 people per room in 2017, with a decrease of 35.71% (Figure 2-34).

Compared with 2016, the year-on-year decreases of two-star and three star-rated hotels in staff to room ratio in 2017 were 2.00% and 12.50%, respectively. One star-rated hotel increased by 14.29% year-on-year.

Figure 2-34   Staff to Room Ratio and its Year-on-year Change of Low Star-rated Hotels (2010~2017)

Chapter III

Quarterly Statistical Analysis of Star-rated Hotels in China

In the first quarter of 2017, there were 10,782 star-rated hotels in the statistical survey management system (hereinafter referred to as the system) of the Ministry of Culture and Tourism, and 10,482 of them were reported, with a filling rate of 97.22%. In the second quarter, there were 11,607 star-rated hotels in the system, and 11,240 of them were reported, with a filling rate of 96.84%. In the third quarter, there were 11,492 star-rated hotels in the system, and 11,266 were reported, with a filling rate of 98.03%. In the fourth quarter, there were 10,962 star-rated hotels in the system, and 10,735 hotels were filled, with a filling rate of 97.93%.

I. Overall Quarterly Situation of Star-rated Hotels in China, 2017

1. Scale and Composition of Operational Revenue

In each quarter of 2017, the Operational Revenue of national star-rated hotels increased steadily, from 47.621 billion yuan in the first quarter to 57.770 billion yuan in the fourth quarter, increased by 10.149 billion yuan, up by 21.31%. Among them, the first quarter was 4.12% lower than the previous year, and the rest quarters increased year-on-year, with the growth rate of 0.39% in the second quarter, 3.87% in the third quarter and 6.13% in the fourth quarter (Figure 3-1).

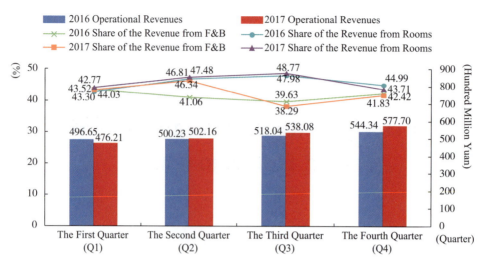

Figure 3-1   The Revenue and Composition of Hotels with Star-rated Hotels (2016~2017)

In 2017, from the perspective of the operational revenue structure of the star-rated hotels in each quarter, the proportion of other operational revenue was basically in the same trend except that the proportion of food and beverage revenue in the second quarter of 2017 showed curve fluctuations. The proportion of the room revenue gradually increased from the first quarter to the third quarter, and fell in the fourth quarter. The proportion of food and beverage revenue gradually decreased from the first to the third quarter, and recovered in the fourth quarter.

In 2017, the proportion of room revenue in the national star-rated hotel operational revenue was on the whole rising, with the year-on-year growth rate of 2.95% in the first quarter, 1.43% in the second quarter and 1.65% in the third quarter, and the year-on-year decrease of 2.85% in the fourth quarter. The proportion of food and beverage operational revenue on the whole shows a downward trend. Except the second quarter's year-on-year growth of 12.86%, the first quarter, the third quarter and the fourth quarter's year-on-year decrease of 0.51%, 3.38% and 1.39% respectively.

2. Operational Conditions

In each quarter of 2017, the average occupancy rate of star-rated hotels in China showed a consistent trend, with a steady rise from the first quarter to the third quarter and a slight recovery in the fourth quarter. In 2017, the average occupancy rate of star-rated hotels in China was the lowest in the first quarter, at 50.20%, increasing by 1.26 per cent year-on-year, with an increase of 2.57%. The average occupancy rate in the second quarter was 56.19%, increasing by 0.89 per cent year-on-year, with an increase of 1.61%. The average occupancy rate was the highest in the third quarter, at 60.58%, increasing by 2.05 per cent year-on-year and increasing by 3.50%. The average occupancy rate in the fourth quarter was 57.71%, increasing by 1.11per cent year-on-year, with an increase of 1.96% (Figure 3-2).

Figure 3-2   The Operational Conditions of Hotels with Star-rated Hotels (2016~2017)

In 2016 the average daily rates rose in the first quarter and declined in the second to the fourth quarter. Different from this characteristic in 2016, the average daily rates of the star-rated hotels in 2017 in each quarter showed year-on-year increase respectively, increased by 4.82 yuan per room night, 7.21 yuan per room night, 13.09 yuan per room night and 11.10 yuan per room night, increased by 1.44%, 2.21%, 4.00% and 3.25% respectively.

In terms of the revenue per available room, in each quarter of 2017, the revenue per available room of the star-rated hotel is basically consistent with the change characteristics of the annual rental rate, showing the overall characteristics of slight recovery after a steady increase. The first quarter saw the lowest revenue per available room, which was

170.60 yuan per room night. The second quarter was 187.40 yuan per room night. The third and fourth quarters were 206.12 yuan per room night and 203.28 yuan per room night, respectively. In terms of variation trend, the revenue per available room for rent had a year-on-year increase in each quarter in 2017 compared with that in 2016, among which the gap was the largest in the third quarter, increasing by 14.62 yuan per room night, an increase of 7.63%. The gap was the smallest in the second quarter, with a year-on-year increase of 6.97 yuan per room night and a growth rate of 3.86%.

II. Research on China's Star-rated Hotels Market: Q1 2017

1. Scale and Composition of Revenue

In the first quarter of 2017, China's star-rated hotels achieved operational revenue of 47.621 billion yuan. Among them, the food and beverage revenue was 20.619 billion yuan, accounting for 43.30% of the operational revenue. The room revenue was 20.965 billion yuan, accounting for 44.03% of the operational revenue (Figure 3-3).

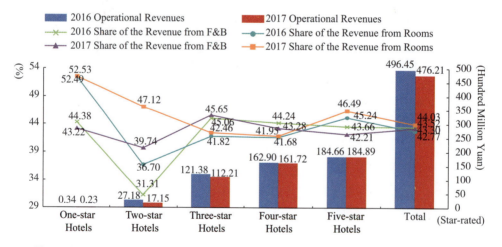

Figure 3-3   The Revenue and Composition of Star-rated Hotels (Q1,2016 and 2017)

In the first quarter of 2017, the operational revenue of five star-rated hotels was the highest, accounting for 18.489 billion yuan, accounting for 38.83% of the total revenue of star-rated hotels in China. Then, the four star-rated hotel achieved a total revenue of 16.172 billion yuan, accounting for 33.96%. The three star-rated hotel achieved a total operational revenue of 11.221 billion yuan, accounting for 23.56%; the total operational revenue of one and two star-rated hotels reached 1.738 billion yuan, accounting for 3.65%.

In terms of the operational revenue structure of the all star-rated hotel, in the first quarter of 2017, the room revenue of five star-rated hotels accounted for 46.49% of the total revenue, and that of food and beverage accounted for 42.21%. Four star-rated hotel room revenue ratio 41.95%, food and beverage revenue accounted for 43.28%; the room revenue of three star-rated hotel is 42.46%, and the revenue of food and beverage is 45.65%. The room revenue of two star-rated hotel is 47.12%, and that of food and beverage is 39.74%. The room revenue of one star-rated hotel accounted for 52.53%, and food and beverage accounted for 43.22%. The proportion of the revenue of one-star, two-star and five-star rated hotels exceeds the proportion of the revenue of food and beverage, while that of three-star and four star-rated hotels exceeds the proportion of the room revenue. Compared with the same period in 2016, the proportion of food and beverage revenue in one-star, four-star and five star-rated hotels decreased year-on-year, respectively by 1.16, 0.96 and 1.45 per cent, with the decreases of 2.61%, 2.17% and 3.32%. The proportion of the food and beverage revenue of two star and three star hotels increased by 8.43 and 0.59 per cent year-on -year, with increases of 26.92% and 1.31%, respectively. The proportion of rooms revenue of all star-rated hotels increased year-on-year, with the increase of 0.04, 10.42, 0.64, 0.27 and 1.25 per cent, respectively, with increases of 0.08%, 28.39%, 1.53%, 0.65% and 2.76% respectively from one to five star rated hotels.

2. Operational Conditions

In the first quarter of 2017, the average occupancy rate of star-rated hotels in China was 50.20%, the average daily rate was 339.87 yuan per room night, and the revenue per available room was 170.60 yuan per room night.

Compared with the same period in 2016, the average occupancy rate of star-rated hotels in the first quarter of 2017 increased by 1.26 per cent, with an increase of 2.57%, among which five star-rated hotels saw the largest increase, increasing by 2.71 per cent, with an increase of 5.14%. There were also increases of different degrees in the two to four star-rated hotels, with increases of 0.50, 0.37 and 1.34 per cent, respectively, with increases of 1.05%, 0.79% and 2.72%. One star-rated hotels showed a downward trend, with a decrease of 1.62 per cent and a decrease of 3.50%.

Compared with the same period in 2016, the average daily rate of star-rated hotels in the first quarter of 2017 increased by 4.82 yuan per room night, an increase of 1.44%, among which five star-rated hotels showed a downward trend, with a decrease of 13.85 yuan per room night, a decrease of 2.18%.

Compared with the same period in 2016, in the first quarter of 2017, the revenue per available room for rent of star-rated hotels in China increased by 6.62 yuan per room night, an increase of 4.04%, among which five star-rated hotels increased the most, by 9.53 yuan per room night, an increase of 2.84% year-on-year. Two to four star-rated hotels also increased in different degrees, with increases of 0.68 yuan per room night, 0.81 yuan per room night and 1.94 yuan per room night respectively, with year-on-year increases of 0.91%, 0.79% and 1.18%, respectively. Same with the average occupancy rate, the rental revenue of one star-rated hotel is also on a downward trend, down by 10.22 yuan per room night, down by 17.70% (Figure 3-4).

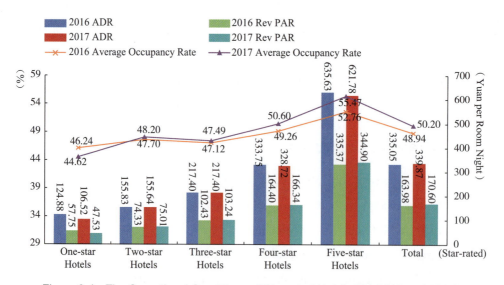

Figure 3-4   The Operational Conditions of Star-rated Hotels (Q1,2016 and 2017)

III. Research on China's Star-rated Hotels Market: Q2 2017

1. Scale and Composition of Revenue

In the second quarter of 2017, the national star-rated hotels achieved the operational revenue of 50.216 billion yuan, among which the food and beverage revenue was 23.27 billion yuan, accounting for 46.34% of the operational revenue. The room revenue was 23.843 billion yuan, accounting for 47.48% of operational revenue (Figure 3-5).

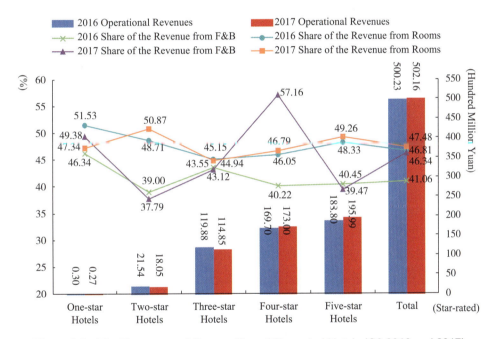

Figure 3-5   The Revenue and Composition of Star-rated Hotels (Q2,2016 and 2017)

In the second quarter of 2017, the operational revenue of all star-rated hotels increased compared with that of the first quarter, among which the five star-rated hotels had the highest operational revenue of 19.599 billion yuan in the second quarter, accounting for 39.03% of the total operational revenue of star-rated hotels. Secondly, the four star-rated hotel achieved a total revenue of 17.30 billion yuan, accounting for 34.45%; The three star-rated hotel achieved a total revenue of 11.485 billion yuan, accounting for 22.87%.

The total revenue of the one star-rated and two star-rated hotels reached 1.832 billion yuan, accounting for 3.65%.

In terms of the operational revenue structure of all star-rated hotels, in the second quarter of 2017, the room revenue of two star-rated hotels accounted for the largest proportion, accounting for 50.87%, and the revenue proportion gap was also the largest, 13.08 per cent higher than that of food and beverage revenue. The gap between the revenue of three star-rated hotels was the smallest, and the proportion of room revenue was only 1.82 per cent higher than that of food and beverage revenue. The proportion of four star-rated hotels' food and beverage revenue exceeded the proportion of room revenue by 10.37 per cent. The proportion of five star-rated hotel room revenue exceeded the proportion of food and beverage revenue by 9.79 per cent; The proportion of the average room revenue of all star-rated hotel was 1.14 per cent higher than that of the food and beverage revenue. Compared with the same period in 2016, the proportion of the average room revenue and food and beverage revenue has increased, with the year-on-year growth of 1.43% and 12.86% respectively, and the gap between them tends to reduce.

2. Operational Conditions

In the second quarter of 2017, the average occupancy rate of national star-rated hotels was 56.19%, the average daily rate was 333.50 yuan per room night, and the revenue per available room was 187.40 yuan per room night.

Compared with the same period in 2016, the average occupancy rate of star-rated hotels in the second quarter of 2017 increased by 0.89 per cent, with increases of 1.61%. Among them, four-star and five star-rated hotels showed different degrees of increase, increasing by 1.71 and 1.93 per cent, respectively, with an increase of 3.02% and 3.25%, respectively. One to three star-rated hotels showed a downward trend, with decreases of 2.85, 1.15 and 0.1 per cent, with decreases of 6.27%, 2.17% and 0.19%, respectively.

Compared with the same period in 2016, the average daily rate of star-rated hotels in the second quarter of 2017 increased by 7.21 yuan per room night, with an increase of 2.21%, among which two-star and five star-rated hotels increased by 2.96 yuan per room night and 5.11 yuan per room night, with increases of 1.90% and 0.84%, respectively. One-star, three-star and four star-rated hotels decreased by 3.73 yuan per room night, 2.19 yuan per room night and 0.72 yuan per room night, with the decrease rate of 3.46%, 1.06% and 0.22%, respectively.

Compared with the same period in 2016, in the second quarter of 2017, the revenue per available room for rent of national star-rated hotels increased by 6.97 yuan per room night, with an increase of 3.86%, among which four-star and five star-rated hotels increased by 5.18 yuan per room night and 14.93 yuan per room night, with year-on-year increases of 2.79% and 4.11%, respectively. One to three star-rated hotels decreased by 4.67 yuan per room night, 0.27 yuan per room night and 1.35 yuan per room night, respectively, with decreases of 9.52%, 0.33% and 1.24% (Figure 3-6).

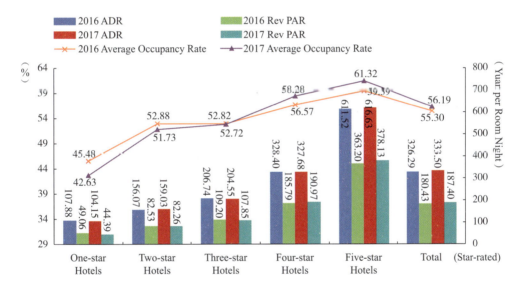

Figure 3-6   The Operational Conditions of Star-rated Hotels (Q2,2016 and 2017)

IV. Research on China's Star-rated Hotels Market: Q3 2017

1. Scale and Composition of Revenue

In the third quarter of 2017, the national star-rated hotels achieved the operational revenue of 53.808 billion yuan, among which the food and beverage revenue was 20.603 billion yuan, accounting for 38.29% of the operational revenue. The room revenue was 26.242 billion yuan, accounting for 48.77% of the operational revenue (Figure 3-7).

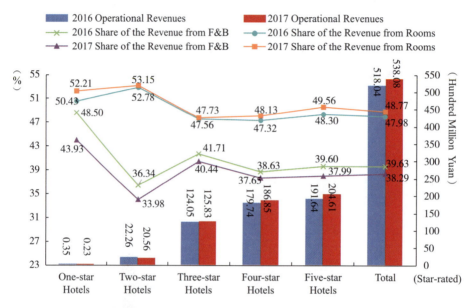

Figure 3-7   The Revenue and Composition of Star-rated Hotels (Q3,2016 and 2017)

In the third quarter of 2017, all star-rated hotels, except one-star ones, saw the operational revenue increase compared with the second quarter, among which five star-rated hotels had the highest operational revenue of 20.461 billion yuan, accounting for 38.03% of the total operational revenue of star-rated hotels in China. Secondly, the four star-rated hotel achieved a total revenue of 18.685 billion yuan, accounting for 34.73%. The three star-rated hotel achieved a total revenue of 12.583 billion yuan, accounting for 23.38%. The total operational revenue of the first and two star-rated hotels reached 2.079 billion yuan, accounting for 3.86%.

According to the operational revenue structure of all star-rated hotels, the room revenue of five star-rated hotels accounted for 49.56% in the third quarter of 2017, while that of food and beverage accounted for 37.99%. The room revenue of four star-rated hotel is 48.13%, and that of food and beverage is 37.65%. The room revenue of three star-rated hotel is 47.73%, and the revenue of food and beverage is 40.44%. The room revenue of two star-rated hotel is 53.15%, and that of food and beverage is 33.98%. The room revenue of one star-rated hotel accounted for 52.21%, and that of food and beverage accounted for 43.93%. In general, the proportion of room revenue exceeded the proportion of food and beverage revenue. Compared with the same period in of 2016, the proportion of food and beverage revenue in one star-rated to five star-rated hotels decreased year-on-year, which decreased by 4.57, 2.36, 1.27, 0.98 and 1.61 per cent, respectively, which decreased by 9.42%, 6.49%, 3.04%, 2.54% and 4.07% respectively. The proportion of the room revenue of all star-rated hotels increased year-on-year, respectively 1.78, 0.37, 0.17, 0.81 and 1.26 per cent, respectively, the increase was 3.53%, 0.70%, 0.36%, 1.71% and 2.61%, respectively.

2. Operational Conditions

In the third quarter of 2017, the average occupancy rate of national star-rated hotels was 60.58%, the average daily rate was 340.25 yuan per room night, and the rental revenue per available room was 206.12 yuan per room night.

Compared with the same period in 2016, the average occupancy rate of star-rated hotels increased by 2.05 per cent in the third quarter of 2017, with an increase of 3.50%. Among them, five star-rated hotels increased by 2.55 per cent year-on-year, with an increase of 4.10%. Two to four star-rated hotels increased by 2.70, 1.00 and 1.57 per cent, respectively, with growth rates of 4.48%, 1.77% and 2.90%, respectively. One star-rated hotels dropped 0.37 per cent year-on-year, with a decrease of 0.83%.

Compared with the same period in 2016, the average daily rate of star-rated hotels in the third quarter of 2017 increased by 13.09 yuan per room night and increased by 4%, among which, two to five star-rated hotels increased by 9.08 yuan per room night, 7.26 yuan per room night, 1.45 yuan per room night and 14.02 yuan per room night, increased by 5.41%, 3.42%, 0.44% and 2.35%, respectively. One star-rated hotels dropped 29.19 yuan per room night, a decrease of 22.86%.

Compared with the same period in 2016, in the third quarter of 2017 the national hotel each available for rental revenue increased 14.62 yuan per room night and increased by 7.63%. Among them, two to five star-rated hotel year-on-year increased 7.68 yuan per room night, 6.28 yuan per room night, 9.90 yuan per room night and 24.31 yuan per room night, increased by 8.47%, 5.25%, 4.93% and 6.54%, respectively. The one star-rated hotel fell by 13.37 yuan per room night, with a decrease of 23.50% (Figure. 3-8).

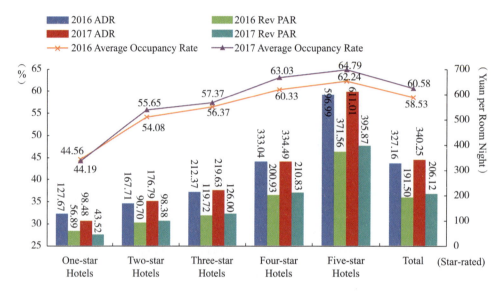

Figure 3-8   The Operational Conditions of Star-rated Hotels (Q3,2016 and 2017)

V. Research on China's Star-rated Hotels Market: Q4 2017

1. Scale and Composition of Revenue

In the fourth quarter of 2017, the national star-rated hotels achieved the operational revenue of 57.77 billion yuan, among which the room revenue was 25.251 billion yuan, accounting for 43.71% of the operational revenue. The food and beverage revenue was 24.165 billion yuan, accounting for 41.83% of the operational revenue (Figure 3-9).

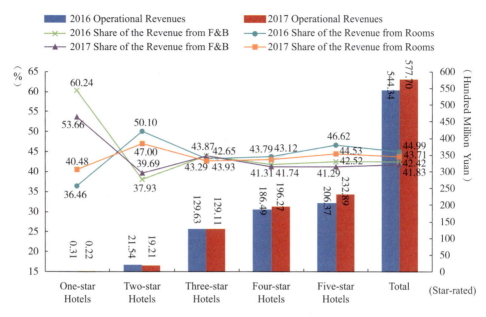

Figure 3-9   The Revenue and Composition of Star-rated Hotels (Q4,2016 and 2017)

In the fourth quarter of 2017, all star-rated hotels, except one-star and two-star ones, increased their operational revenue compared with that of the third quarter, among which five star-rated hotels had the highest operational revenue of 23.289 billion yuan, accounting for 40.31% of the total national star-rated hotels. Secondly, the four star-rated hotel achieved a total revenue of 19.627 billion yuan, accounting for 33.97%. The three star-rated hotel achieved a total operational revenue of 12.911 billion yuan, accounting for 22.35%. The total operational revenue of the first star-rated and two star-rated hotels was 1.943 billion yuan, accounting for 3.36%.

In terms of to the operational revenue structure of star-rated hotels, the room revenue of five star-rated hotels accounted for 44.53% and the food and beverage revenue accounted for 41.29% in the fourth quarter of 2017. The room revenue of four star-rated hotels accounts for 43.12%, food and beverage revenue accounts for 41.31%; The room revenue of three star-rated hotel accounted for 42.65%, and the revenue of food and beverage accounted for 43.87%. The room revenue of two star-rated hotel is 47% and the revenue of food and beverage is 39.69%. The room revenue of one star-rated hotel is 40.48%, and the revenue of food and beverage is 53.66%. The gravity of one star-rated hotel operation tends to center on food and beverage, the gravity of two star-rated hotel operational tends to center on room, the proportion of food and beverage and room revenue of other star-rated hotels is relatively balanced. Compared with the same period in 2016, the proportion of food and beverage revenue in one-star, three-star, four-star and five star-rated hotels decreased year-on-year, decreasing by 6.58, 0.06, 0.43 and 1.23 per cent respectively, decreasing by 10.92%, 0.14%, 1.03% and 2.89% respectively. The proportion of the food and beverage revenue of two star-rated hotels increased by 1.76 per cent, increased by 4.64%. The proportion of room revenue in the two to five star-rated hotels decreased year-on-year by 3.10, 0.64, 0.67 and 2.09 per cent, respectively, with decreases of 6.19%, 1.48%, 1.53% and 4.48% respectively. The revenue of one star-rated hotel increased by 4.02 per cent, the increase was 11.03%.

2. Operational Conditions

In the fourth quarter of 2017, the average occupancy rate of national star-rated hotels was 57.71%, the average daily rate was 352.23 yuan per room night, and the revenue per available room was 203.28 yuan per room night.

Compared with the same period in 2016, the average occupancy rate of star-rated hotels in the fourth quarter of 2017 increased by 1.11 per cent, with an increase of 1.96%, among which five star-rated hotels increased by 2.12 per cent year-on-year, with an increase of 3.44%. One-star, three-star and four star-rated hotels increased by 0.74, 0.26 and 1.08 per cent year-on-year, respectively, with increases of 1.70%, 0.49% and 1.85%. Two star-rated hotels fell 2% year-on-year, a decrease of 3.66%.

Compared with the same period in 2016, the average daily rate of star-rated hotels in the fourth quarter of 2017 increased by 11.10 yuan per room night, with an increase of 3.25%. Among them, three to five star-rated to five star-rated hotels increased by 5.23 yuan per room night, 0.71 yuan per room night and 19.12 yuan per room night, with year-on-year increases of 2.39%, 0.21% and 3.11%, respectively. One-star and two star-rated hotels dropped by 12.28 yuan per room night and 13.76 yuan per room night, respectively, down by 12.04% and 7.60%, respectively.

Compared with the same period in 2016, the revenue per available room for rent in the fourth quarter of 2017 increased by 10.21 yuan per room night, an increase of 5.29%, among which three star-rated to five star-rated hotels increased by 3.37 yuan per room night, 4.04 yuan per room night and 25.24 yuan per room night, increases of 2.88%, 2.06% and 6.67%, respectively. One-star and two star-rated hotels decreased by 4.66 yuan per room night and 7.43 yuan per room night, respectively, with a decrease of 10.52% and 7.95% (Figure 3-10).

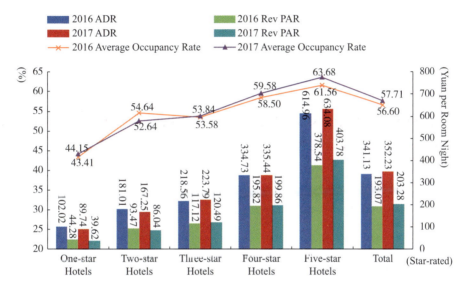

Figure 3-10   The Operational Conditions of Star-rated Hotels (Q4,2016 and 2017)

Chapter IV

Analysis of the Regional Market of China's Star-rated Hotel Industry

I. Overall Situation of Regional Market of China's Star-rated Hotels in 2017

1. Distribution of Star-rated Hotels by Numbers

According to the distribution of the number of star-rated hotels in 2017, east China has the largest number, while northeast China has the smallest number. Specifically, the number of star-rated hotels in north China, northeast China, east China, south China, central China, southwest China and northwest China are 1359, 638, 2,508, 1,148, 1,400, 1,331 and 1,182, accounting for 14.21%, 6.67%, 26.22%, 12%, 14.64%, 13.91% and 12.36% respectively (Figure 4-1).

Compared with 2016, the number of north China increased the most and the number of northeast China decreased the most. Specifically, the number of star-rated hotels in north China and northwest increased by 140 and 92, respectively, by 11.48% and 8.44% year-on-year. The number of star-rated hotels in northeast China, east China, south China, central China and southwest China decreased by 78, 199, 109, 84 and 57, respectively, and the decrease was 10.89%, 7.35%, 8.67%, 5.66% and 4.11%, respectively.

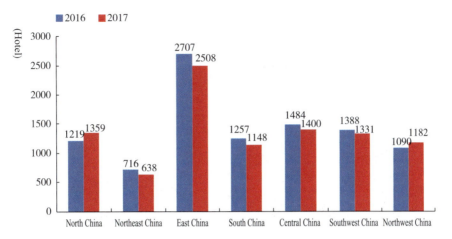

Figure 4-1   Quantitive Distribution of Star-rated Hotels in Different Regions (2016 and 2017)

2. Distribution of Star-rated Hotels by Revenue

(1) Operational Revenue

In terms of the operational revenue of star-rated hotels in 2017, east China has the highest revenue while northeast China has the least. North China, northeast China, east China, south China, central China, southwest and northwest area hotel operational revenue is 39.688 billion yuan, 8.13 billion yuan, 81.456 billion yuan, 29.401 billion yuan, 20.318 billion yuan, 17.525 billion yuan and 11.875 billion yuan respectively, accounting for 19.04%, 3.90%, 39.09%, 14.11%, 9.75%, 8.41% and 5.70% respectively (Figure 4-2)

Compared with 2016, except for the south China, other regions hotel revenues tend to rise, the north China, northeast China, east China, central China, southwest and northwest area hotel revenue has year-on-year increases of 2.444 billion yuan, 182 million yuan, 1.537 billion yuan, 257 million yuan, 993 million yuan and 318 million yuan, respectively, up by 6.56%, 2.29%, 1.92%, 1.28%, 6.01% and 2.75% respectively; operational revenue in south China fell by 640 million yuan, and down by 0.22%, year-on-year

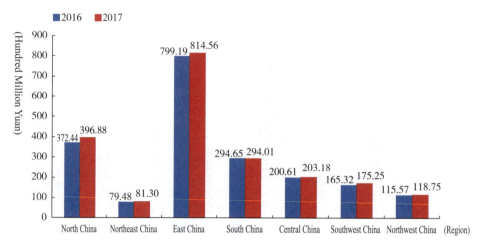

Figure 4-2   Distribution of Operational Revenues of Star-rated Hotels in Different

Regions (2016 and 2017)

(2) Operational Revenue of Each Hundred-Yuan Fixed Asset

The annual fixed assets of star-rated hotels reached operational revenue of each hundred-yuan in 2017, with the largest amount in east China at 48.14 yuan. The least in northeast China was 29.39 yuan. In north China, south China, central China, southwest China and northwest China, the operational revenue of each hundred-yuan fixed assets of star-rated hotels was 33.78 yuan, 45.83 yuan, 42.09 yuan, 32.76 yuan and 33.16 yuan respectively (Figure 4-3).

Compared with 2016, except for the north China, other regions hotels' operational revenue of each hundred-yuan fixed assets tend to rise, while that of northeast, east China, south China, central China, southwest and northwest China's hotel increased 2.32 yuan, 0.94 yuan, 7.88 yuan, 1.64 yuan, 0.40 yuan and 0.72 yuan, respectively, up by 8.57%, 1.99%, 20.76%, 4.05%, 1.24% and 2.22%, respectively. In north China, the operational revenue of each hundred-yuan fixed assets of star-rated hotels decreased 1.74 yuan and down by 4.90%.

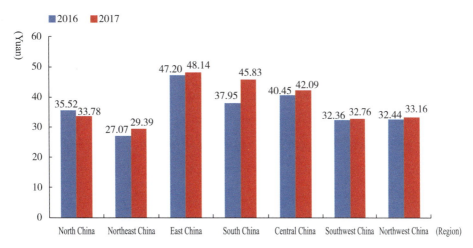

Figure 4-3   Operational Revenues of Each Hundred-yuan Fixed Assets of Star-rated Hotels in Different Regions (2016 and 2017)

(3) Operational Revenues per Room

In 2017, the operational revenue per room in the star-rated hotels was the highest in east China, with 197,100 yuan. The least in northwest China was 84,000 yuan. The operational revenue per room of star-rated hotels in north China, northeast China, south China, central China and southwest China was 139,100 yuan, 95,000 yuan, 154,600 yuan, 107,100 yuan and 106,000 yuan respectively (Figure 4-4).

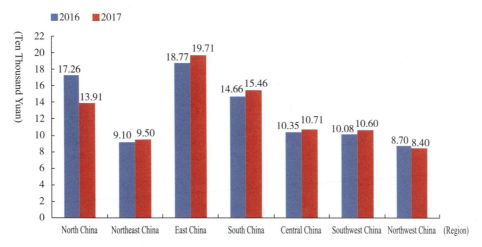

Figure 4-4   Operational Revenues of Each Room of Star-rated Hotels in Different Regions (2016 and 2017)

145

Compared with 2016, each room of star-rated hotels in all regions except north China and northwest China showed an upward trend in operational revenue. Specifically, the operational revenue per room of star-rated hotels in northeast China, east China, south China, central China and southwest China increased by 4,000 yuan, 9,400 yuan, 8,000 yuan, 3,600 yuan and 5,200 yuan, respectively, increasing by 4.40%, 5.01%, 5.46%, 3.48% and 5.16% year-on-year. The operational revenue per room of star-rated hotels in north China and northwest China decreased by 33,500 yuan and 3,000 yuan, and the decrease was 19.41% and 3.45%, respectively.

(4) Operational Revenues of Each Hundred-yuan Fixed Assets

In 2017, the operational revenues of each hundred-yuan fixed assets, with the largest amount in northeast China, which was 340.21 yuan. The least in east China was 207.74 yuan. In north China, south China, central China, southwest China and northwest China, the operational revenues of each hundred-yuan fixed assets were 296.04 yuan, 218.19 yuan, 237.59 yuan, 305.28 yuan and 301.61 yuan respectively (Figure 4-5).

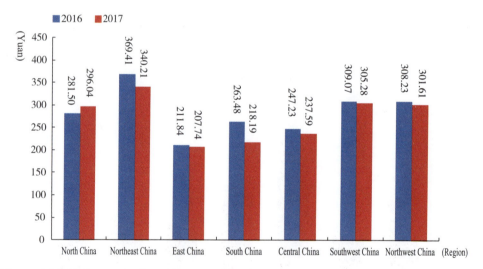

Figure 4-5   Fix Assets for Each Hundred-Yuan Operational Revenues of Star-rated Hotels in Different Regions (2016 and 2017)

Compared with 2016, the occupancy of fixed assets of each hundred-yuan of operational revenue of star-rated hotels in all regions except north China showed a downward trend. Specifically, in the northeast, east China, south China, central China, southwest and northwest regions, the occupancy of each hundred-yuan of operational revenue of star-rated hotels decreased by 29.20 yuan, 4.10 yuan, 45.29 yuan, 9.64 yuan, 3.79 yuan and 6.62 yuan, respectively, down by 7.90%, 1.94%, 17.19%, 3.90%, 1.23% and 2.15% year-on-year. The star-rated hotels in north China increased by 14.54 yuan, or 5.17%, year-on-year.

3. Distribution of Star-rated Hotels by Total Profit

In 2017, the profit level of star-rated hotels in various regions varied greatly. Specifically, east China was the most profitable, with 4.885 billion yuan. It was followed by south China, central China, north China and southwest China, with profits of 2,507 million yuan, 346 million yuan, 243 million yuan and 26 million yuan, respectively. In addition to the five regions mentioned above, all other regions suffered losses of in different degrees, among which the northeast region suffered the most losses, which was 493 million yuan. It was followed by northwest, with a loss of 268 million yuan (Figure 4-6).

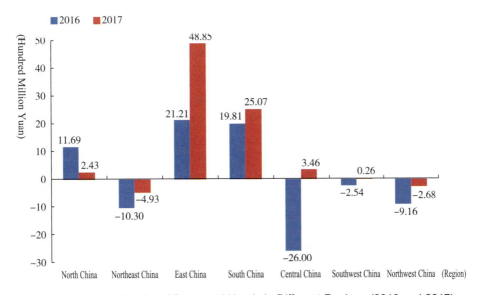

Figure 4-6   Total Profits of Star-rated Hotels in Different Regions (2016 and 2017)

Compared with 2016, central China saw the biggest change, with the annual profit of star-rated hotels increasing by 2.946 billion yuan, an increase of 113.31%. Secondly, in east China, the profit of star-rated hotels increased by 2.764 billion yuan, up by 130.32%. In northwes, northeast, south and southwest China, the profits of star-rated hotels increased by 648 million yuan, 537 million yuan, 526 million yuan and 280 million yuan, respectively, increasing by 70.74%, 52.14%, 26.55% and 110.24%, respectively.

4. Distribution of Star-rated Hotels by Human Resources

The number of star-rated hotel employees in 2017 was the largest in east China with 367,100, down 28,400 and a decrease of 7.18%. In northeast China, the least number was 55,800, with a decrease of 5,000 and a decrease of 8.22% year on year. The number of star-rated hotels in north China was 187,900, up 5,100 and up 2.79% year-on-year. In south China, central China, southwest China and northwest China, the number of star-rated hotel employees was 155,100, 144,800, 126,000 and 88,000 respectively, decreasing by 21,300, 7,900, 6,300and 8,000 respectively year-on-year, and decreasing by 12.07%, 5.17%, 4.76% and 8.33% respectively (Figure 4-7).

The annual star-rated hotel staff to room ratio in 2017 showed a decline in different degrees in all regions. Specifically, east China was the largest, with 0.89 people per room, down 0.04 people per room and a decrease of 4.30%. In the northwestern region, the least number was 0.62 people per room, down by 0.10 people per room, down by 13.89%. In north China, northeast China, south China, central China and southwest China, the ratio of room to room in star-rated hotels was 0.66, 0.65, 0.82, 0.76 and 0.76 people per room respectively, decreasing by 0.19, 0.05, 0.06, 0.03 and 0.05 people per room respectively year-on-year, with the decrease of 22.35%, 7.14%, 6.82%, 3.80% and 6.17% respectively.

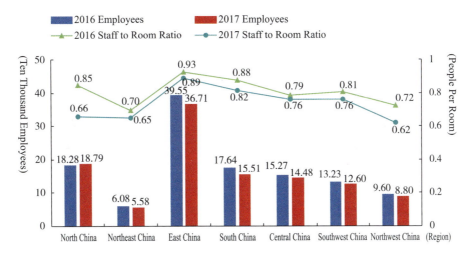

Figure 4-7   The Number of Employees and Staff to Room Ratio of Star-rated Hotels in Different Regions (2016 and 2017)

II. Analysis of Star-rated Hotel Industry in North China (Beijing, Tianjin, Hebei, Shanxi and Inner Mongolia)

1. Distribution of Star-rated Hotels by Numbers

In 2017, there were 1,359 star-rated hotels in north China, mainly three star-rated and four star-rated hotels. Specifically, there are 121 five star-rated hotels, accounting for 8.90% of the total star-rated hotels in north China. There are 367 four star-rated hotels, accounting for 27.01% of the total star-rated hotels in north China. There are 566 three star-rated hotels, accounting for 41.65% of the total in north China. There are 293 two star-rated hotels, accounting for 21.56% of the total star-rated hotels in north China. There are 12 one star-rated hotels in total, accounting for 0.88% of the total star-rated hotels in north China (Figure 4-8).

Compared with 2016, the proportion of five star-rated hotels in north China decreased by 9.55% year-on-year, four star-rated hotels decreased by 7.79% year-on-year, three star-rated hotels decreased by 3.48% year-on-year, two star-rated hotels increased by 23.39%

year-on-year, and one star-rated hotels increased by 258.79% year-on-year.

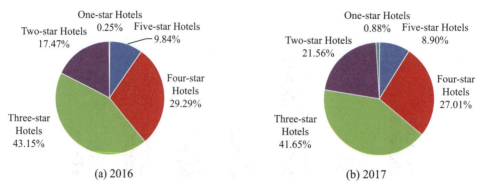

(a) 2016   (b) 2017

Figure 4-8   Distribution of Star-rated Hotels by Numbers in North China (2016 and 2017)

In terms of the distribution of star-rated hotels, there were 496 star-rated hotels in Beijing in 2017, accounting for 36.50% of the star-rated hotels in north China. There are 80 star-rated hotels in Tianjin, accounting for 5.89% of the number of star-rated hotels in north China. There are 338 star-rated hotels in Hebei, accounting for 24.87% of the star-rated hotels in north China. There are 203 star-rated hotels in Shanxi, accounting for 14.94% of the number of star-rated hotels in north China. Inner Mongolia has 242 star-rated hotels, accounting for 17.81% of the number of star-rated hotels in north China.

Compared with 2016, the number of star-rated hotels in Beijing, Shanxi and Inner Mongolia increased by 80, 9 and 67, respectively, and the growth rate was 19.23%, 4.64% and 38.29%, respectively. The number of star-rated hotels in Tianjin and Hebei decreased by 4 and 12, respectively, and the decrease was 4.76% and 3.43% (Figure 4-9).

In terms of the distribution structure of star-rated hotels, three star-rated hotels dominated in north China in 2017, followed by four-star, two-star, five-star and one star-rated hotels. Specifically, there are 10, 122, 182, 122 and 60 one star-rated to five star-rated hotels in Beijing, accounting for 2.02%, 24.60%, 36.69%, 24.60% and 12.10% of the total hotels in Beijing. The number of one to five star-rated hotels in Tianjin is 0, 7, 24, 34 and 15 respectively, accounting for 0%, 8.75%, 30.00%, 42.50% and 18.75% of the total hotels in Tianjin respectively. There are 2, 40, 154, 122 and 20 one star-rated to five star-rated hotels in Hebei, accounting for 0.59%, 11.83%, 45.56%, 36.09% and 5.92% of the total hotels in Hebei. The number of one to five star-rated hotels in Shanxi is 0, 30, 104, 53 and 16 respectively, accounting for 0%, 14.78%, 51.23%, 26.11% and 7.88% of the total hotels in Shanxi respectively. The number of one to five star-rated hotels in Inner Mongolia is 0, 94, 102, 36 and 10 respectively, accounting for 0%, 38.84%, 42.15%, 14.88% and 4.13% of the total number of hotels in Inner Mongolia respectively.

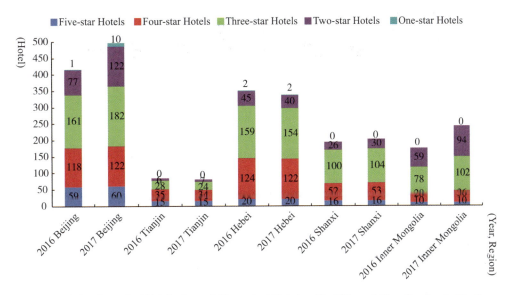

Figure 4-9   Quantity Distribution of Star-rated Hotels with Different Star Grades in North China (2016 and 2017)

2. Distribution of Star-rated Hotels by Revenue

(1) Operational Revenue and its Composition

In 2017, the operational revenue of star-rated hotels in north China reached 39.688 billion yuan, increasing by 6.56% year-on-year, among which the room revenue was 18.375 billion yuan, accounting for 46.30% of the operational revenue of star-rated hotels in north China. Food and beverage revenue was 13.556 billion yuan, accounting for 34.16% of the operational revenue of star-rated hotels in north China. Other revenue was 7.757 billion yuan, accounting for 19.54% of the operational revenue of star-rated hotels in north China (Figure 4-10).

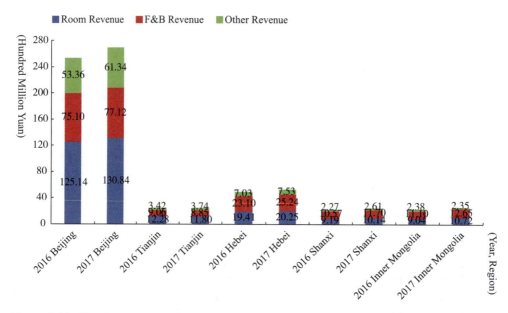

Figure 4-10   The Revenue and Composition of Star-rated Hotels in North China (2016 and 2017)

In north China in 2017, the operational revenue of Beijing, Tianjin, Hebei, Shanxi and Inner Mongolia was 26.93 billion yuan, 2.439 billion yuan, 5.302 billion yuan, 2.444 billion yuan and 2.572 billion yuan, accounting for 67.86%, 6.15%, 13.36%, 6.16% and 6.48% respectively, with Beijing taking the largest share. Compared with 2016, the operational revenue of Beijing, Hebei, Shanxi and Inner Mongolia increased year-on-year, with growth rates of 6.19%, 7.04%, 10.98% and 14.24% respectively. Operational revenue in Tianjin dropped by 1.52% year-on-year.

The operational revenue structure of star-rated hotels in north China in 2017 is mainly dominated by the revenue from rooms and food and beverage, accounting for 80.46% of the total revenue. To be specific, consistent with the performance rule in 2016, the operational revenue of Beijing and Tianjin star-rated hotels is mainly dominated by room revenue, accounting for 48.59% and 48.38% of the total operational revenue respectively. The operational revenue of Hebei, Shanxi and Inner Mongolia is mainly dominated by food and beverage revenue, accounting for 47.61%, 47.86% and 49.17% of the total operational revenue respectively (Table 4-1).

Table 4-1   The Share of Operational Revenues of Star-rated Hotels in North China (2016~2017)

	Room Revenue (%)		Food and beverage Revenue (%)		Other Revenue (%)	
	2016	2017	2016	2017	2016	2017
North China	47.00	46.30	34.62	34.16	18.38	19.54
Beijing	49.34	48.59	29.61	28.64	21.04	22.78
Tianjin	49.60	48.38	36.60	36.30	13.80	15.32
Hebei	39.19	38.18	46.63	47.61	14.18	14.21
Shanxi	41.72	41.48	47.99	47.86	10.29	10.66
Inner Mongolia	40.15	41.69	49.29	49.17	10.56	9.14

(2) Operational Revenue of Each Hundred-Yuan Fixed Asset

In terms of the operational revenue of each hundred-yuan fixed assets of star-rated hotels, the annual revenue of north China was 33.78 yuan in 2017, down 1.75 yuan year-on-year, with a decrease of 4.91%. Specifically, the investment in fixed assets of star-rated hotels in Beijing has the strongest earning capacity, which is 38.89 yuan, a year-on-year increase of 0.49 yuan year-on-year and an increase of 1.28%. That of Tianjin was 19.41 yuan, a year-on-year decrease of 30.15 yuan and a decrease of 60.84%. That of Hebei was 33.81 yuan, a year-on-year increase of 2.33 yuan and an increase of 7.44%. That of Shanxi was 26.21 yuan, a year-on-year increase of 0.54 yuan and an increase 2.10%. That of Inner Mongolia was 24.09 yuan, a year-on-year increase of 0.34 yuan and an increase 1.43% (Figure 4-11)

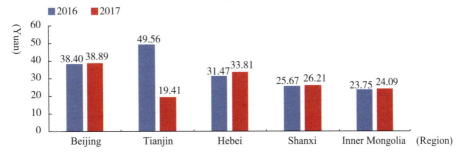

Figure 4-11   Operational Revenues of Each Hundred-yuan Fixed Assets of Star-rated Hotels in North China (2016 and 2017)

(3) Operational Revenues per Room

In terms of the operational revenue per room of the star-rated hotel, the annual revenue in north China was 139,100 yuan in 2017, down 33,400 yuan year-on-year, a decrease of 19.38%. Specifically, Beijing reached 163,800 yuan, a year-on-year decrease of 87,200 yuan, a decrease of 34.74%. Tianjin reached 151,700 yuan, an increase of 3,000 yuan or 2.02% year-on-year. Hebei reached 103,400 yuan, up 5,600 yuan year-on-year, up 5.73%. Shanxi reached 94,300 yuan, an increase of 7,500 yuan, an increase of 8.64%. Inner Mongolia reached 93,300 yuan, 0.84 million yuan less than that of the previous year, with a decrease of 8.26% (Figure 4-12).

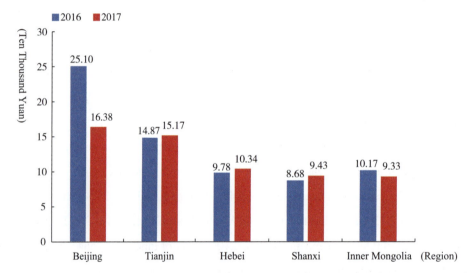

Figure 4-12   Operational Revenues of Per Room of Star-rated Hotels in North China (2016 and 2017)

(4) Fixed Assets for Each Hundred-yuan Operational Revenue

In terms of the fixed assets occupied by each hundred-yuan of operational revenue of star-rated hotels, the annual revenue of north China in 2017 was 296.04 yuan, up 14.54 yuan year-on-year, with an increase of 5.17%. Specifically, Beijing was 257.11 yuan, down 3.32 yuan year-on-year, down 1.27%; Tianjin was 515.16 yuan, up 313.38 yuan year-on-year, up 155.31%. Hebei was 295.81 yuan, a year-on-year decrease of 21.90 yuan and a decrease of 6.89%. Shanxi was 381.48 yuan, down 8.10 yuan and 2.08%. Inner Mongolia was 415.08 yuan, a year-on-year decrease of 6.00 yuan and a decrease of 1.42% (Figure 4-13).

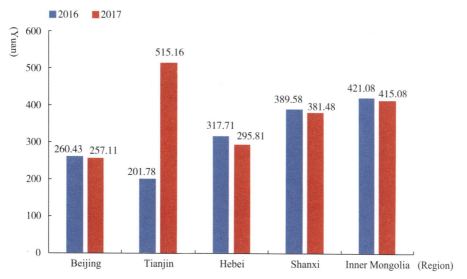

Figure 4-13   Fix Assets for Each Hundred-Yuan Operational Revenues of Star-rated Hotels in North China (2016 and 2017)

3. Distribution of Star-rated Hotels by Total Profit

The annual profit of north China in 2017 was 243 million yuan, down by 927 million yuan, or 79.24% year-on-year in terms of the annual total profit of star-rated hotels. Specifically, only Beijing has been profitable in recent two years, while other regions are losing profits. Total profit in Beijing was 1.588 billion yuan, down by 1.158 billion yuan, or 42.17% year-on-year. Tianjin lost 80 million yuan, a decrease of year-on-year loss of 74 million yuan, a reduction of 48.05%; Hebei posted a loss of 727 million yuan, an increase of year-on-year loss of 94 million yuan or 14.85%. Shanxi lost 377 million yuan, a decrease of year-on-year loss of 74 million yuan, a reduction of 16.41%. Inner Mongolia posted a loss of 162 million yuan, with a decrease of year-on-year loss of 177 million yuan and a reduction of 52.21% (Figure 4-14)

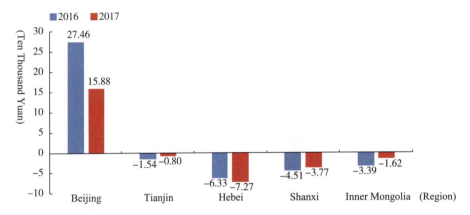

Figure 4-14   Total Profits of Star-rated Hotels in North China (2016 and 2017)

4. Distribution of Star-rated Hotels by Human Resources

In terms of the number of star-rated hotel employees, the number of people in north China was 187,900 in 2017, an year-on-year increase of 5,000 and a rise of 2.75%. Specifically, Beijing was 87,600, up by 2,600 year-on-year, an increase of 3.06%. Tianjin saw a drop of 5.11% to 13,000, down by 700 year-on-year. Hebei was 42,700, up by 3,000 and 0.71% year-on-year. Shanxi was 24,300, down by 200 year-on-year and a decrease of 0.82%. Inner Mongolia was 20,300, up by 3,000 year-on-year, up by 17.34% (Figure 4-15).

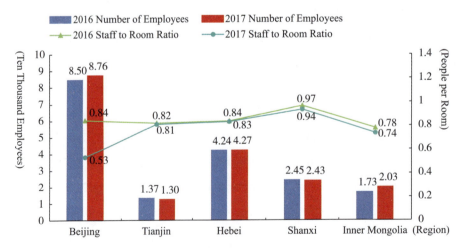

Figure 4-15   The Number of Employees and Staff to Room Ratio of Star-rated Hotels in North China (2016 and 2017)

In terms of the staff to room ratio of star-rated hotels, there were 0.66 people per room in north China in 2017, with a year-on-year decrease of 0.19 people per room and a decrease of 22.26%. Specifically, Beijing had 0.53 people per room, a year-on year decrease of 0.31 people per room, a decrease of 36.90%. Tianjin had 0.81 people per room, a year-on year decrease of 0.01 people per room, a decrease of 1.22%. Hebei had 0.83 people per room, a year-on year decrease of 0.01 people per room, a decrease of 1.19%. Shanxi had 0.94 people per room, 0.03 people per room, a decrease of 3.09%. Inner Mongolia had 0.74 people per room, a year-on year decrease of 0.04 people per room, a decrease of 5.13%.

III. Analysis of Star-rated Hotel Industry in Northeast China (Heilongjiang, Jilin and Liaoning)

1. Distribution of Star-rated Hotels by Numbers

In 2017, there were 638 star-rated hotels in northeast China, mainly three star-rated and four star-rated hotels. Specifically, there are 35 five star rated hotels, accounting for 5.49% of the total star-rated hotels in northeast China. There are 149 four star-rated hotels in total, accounting for 23.35% of the total star-rated hotels in northeast China. There are 338 three star-rated hotels in total, accounting for 52.98% of the total five star-rated hotels in northeast China. There are 114 two star-rated hotels, accounting for 17.87% of the total in northeast China. There are 2 one star-rated hotels in total, accounting for 0.31% of the total star-rated hotels in northeast China (Figure 4-16).

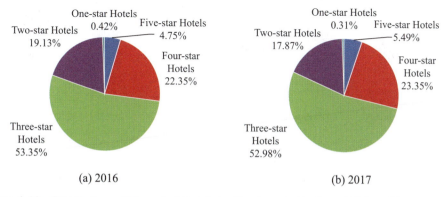

(a) 2016   (b) 2017

Figure 4-16   Distribution of Star-rated Hotels by Numbers in Northeast China (2016 and 2017)

Compared with 2016, the proportion of five star-rated hotels in northeast China increased by 15.53%, four star-rated hotels increased by 4.51%, three star-rated hotels decreased by 0.70%, two-star hotels decreased by 6.62% and one star-rated hotels decreased by 25.18%.

In terms of the distribution of star-rated hotels, there were 187 star-rated hotels in Heilongjiang in 2017, accounting for 29.31% of the number of star-rated hotels in northeast China. There were 115 star-rated hotels in Jilin, accounting for 18.03% of the star-rated hotels in northeast China. There were 336 star-rated hotels in Liaoning, accounting for 52.66% of the star-rated hotels in northeast China.

Compared with 2016, the number of star-rated hotels in Heilongjiang, Jilin and Liaoning all showed a downward trend year-on-year, down by 11, 54 and 13 respectively, and the reduction was 5.56%, 31.95% and 3.72% respectively (Figure 4-17).

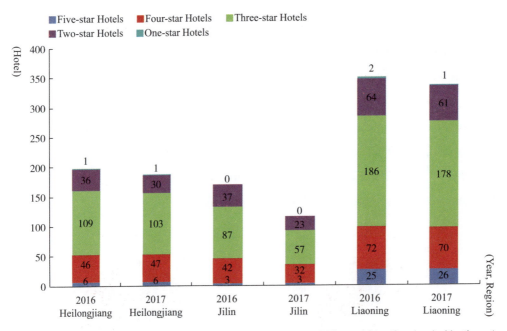

Figure 4-17   Quantity Distribution of Star-rated Hotels with Different Star Grades in Northeast China (2016 and 2017)

In terms of the distribution structure of the number of star-rated hotels, three star-rated hotels dominated the northeast China in 2017, followed by four-star, two-star, five-star and one star-rated hotels. Specifically, Heilongjiang has 1, 30, 103, 47 and 6 one star-ratedto five star-rated hotels, accounting for 0.53%, 16.04%, 55.08%, 25.13% and 3.12% of its total hotels. The number of one to five star-rated to five star-rated hotels in Jilin is 0, 23, 57, 32 and 3, respectively, accounting for 0%, 20.00%, 49.57%, 27.83% and 2.61% of of its total hotels in Jilin. There are 1, 61, 178, 70 and 26 one star-ratedto five star-rated hotels in Liaoning, accounting for 0.30%, 18.15%, 52.98%, 20.83% and 7.74% respectively.

2. Distribution of Star-rated Hotels by Revenue

(1) Operational Revenue and its Composition

In 2017, the annual operational revenue of star-rated hotels in northeast China reached 8.103 billion yuan, increasing by 2.29% year-on-year, of which 3.775 billion yuan was realized by room revenue, accounting for 46.43% of the operational revenue of star-rated hotels in northeast China. Food and beverage revenue reached 3.22 billion yuan, accounting for 39.61% of the operational revenue of star-rated hotels in northeast China; Other revenue was 1.135 billion yuan, accounting for 13.96% of the operational revenue of starred hotels in northeast China (Figure 4-18).

Figure 4-18 The Revenue and Composition of Star-rated Hotels in Northeast China (2016 and 2017)

In northeast China in 2017, Heilongjiang, Jilin and Liaoning accounted for 1.606 billion yuan, 1.445 billion yuan and 5.08 billion yuan, respectively, accounting for 19.74%, 17.77% and 62.49%, with Liaoning taking the largest share. Compared with 2016, the operational revenue of Heilongjiang and Jilin decreased by 13.21% and 6.07%, respectively. Liaoning's operational revenue increased by 11.40% year-on-year.

The operational revenue structure of star-rated hotels in northeast China in 2017 is mainly dominated by the revenue from rooms and food and beverage, accounting for 86.04% of the total revenue. Specifically, consistent with the performance in 2016, the room revenue in Heilongjiang and Liaoning star-rated hotels exceeded the food and beverage revenue, accounting for 52.18% and 45.04% of the total operational revenue respectively. The revenue of rooms and food and beverage in Jilin is equivalent, accounting for 44.90% and 44.67% respectively (Table 4-2).

Table 4-2   The Share of Operational Revenues of Star-rated Hotels in Northeast China (2016 and 2017)

	Room Revenue (%)		Food and Beverage Revenue (%)		Other Revenue (%)	
	2016	2017	2016	2017	2016	2017
Northeast China	47.07	46.43	40.84	39.61	12.10	13.96
Heilongjiang	51.26	52.18	34.30	32.45	14.43	15.37
Jilin	45.90	44.90	46.05	44.67	8.05	10.43
Liaoning	45.76	45.04	41.73	40.43	12.51	14.52

(2) Operational Revenue of Each Hundred-Yuan Fixed Asset

In terms of the operational revenue realized by the each hundred-yuan fixed assets of star-rated hotels, the annual revenue of northeast China in 2017 was 29.39 yuan, up by 2.32 yuan year-on-year, with an increase of 8.58%. Specifically, Liaoning star-rated hotel has the highest revenue generating capacity in its investment in fixed assets, which was 31.07 yuan, up 5.28 yuan year-on-year, up 20.47%. Heilongjiang was 27.07 yuan, a year-on-year decrease of 3.88 yuan, a decrease of 12.54%. Jilin was 26.85 yuan, a year-on-year decrease of 0.13 yuan and a decrease of 0.48% (Figure 4-19).

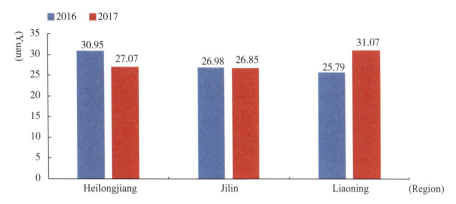

Figure 4-19   Operational Revenues of Each Hundred-yuan Fixed Assets of Star-rated Hotels in Northeast China (2016 and 2017)

(3) Operational Revenues per Room

In terms of the operational revenue per room of the star-rated hotels, the annual revenue in northeast China in 2017 was 95,000 yuan, with an increase of 4,000 yuan year-on-year and an increase of 4.34%. Specifically, Heilongjiang reached 77,500 yuan, with a decrease of 8,700 yuan year-on-year and a decrease of 10.09%. Jilin reached 110,800 yuan, with an increase of 12,800 yuan year-on-year and an increase of 13.06%. Liaoning reached 98,000 yuan, with an increase of 7,100 yuan year-on-year and an increase of 7.81% (Figure 4-20).

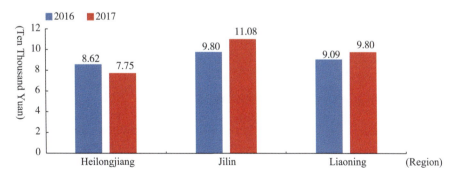

Figure 4-20   Operational Revenues of Per Room of Star-rated Hotels in Northeast China (2016 and 2017)

(4) Fixed Assets for Each Hundred-yuan Operational Revenue

In terms of the fixed assets occupied by each hundred-yuan of operational revenue of star-rated hotels, the annual revenue of northeast China in 2017 was 340.21 yuan, a decrease of 29.20 yuan and a decrease of 7.90% year-on-year. Specifically, Heilongjiang reached 369.41 yuan, with an increase of 46.35 yuan year-on-year and an increase of 14.35%. Jilin reached 372.50 yuan, with an increase of 1.91 yuan year-on-year and an increase of 0.52%. Liaoning reached 321.81 yuan, with a decrease of 66.00 yuan year-on-year and a decrease of 17.02% (Figure 4-21).

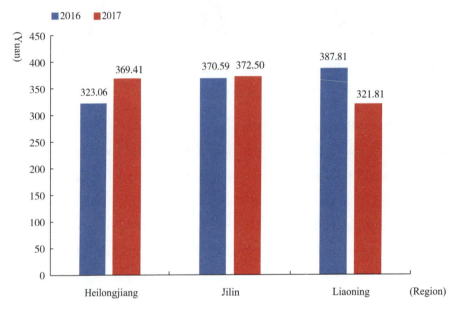

Figure 4-21   Fix Assets for Each Hundred-Yuan Operational Revenues of Star-rated Hotels in Northeast China (2016 and 2017)

3. Distribution of Star-rated Hotels by Total Profit

The annual loss in the northeast region in 2017 was 493 million yuan, a year-on-year decrease of 537 million yuan and a decrease of 52.15% from the annual total profit of star-rated hotels. Specifically, Heilongjiang, Jilin and Liaoning were all in the state of loss, among which Heilongjiang lost 63 million yuan, an increase of loss of 46 million yuan year-on-year, an increase of 270.59%. Jilin lost 161 million yuan, a decrease of loss of 28 million yuan, a decrease of 14.81%. Liaoning lost 269 million yuan, with a decrease of loss of 556 million yuan, a decrease of 67.39% (Figure 4-22).

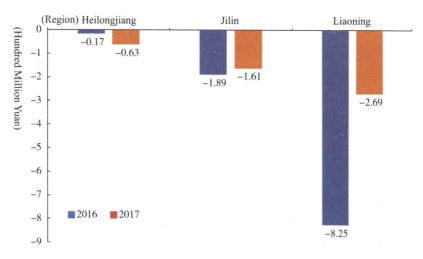

Figure 4-22   Total Profits of Star-rated Hotels in Northeast China (2016 and 2017)

4. Distribution of Star-rated Hotels by Human Resources

In terms of the star-rated hotel employees in northeast China, the number was 53,800 in 2017, down by 5100 year-on-year, down by 8.33%. Specifically, Heilongjiang was 13,300, increased by 300, an increase of 2.31% year-on-year. Jilin was 10,400, a decrease of 3,500 and a decrease of 25.18% year-on-year. Liaoning had 32,100, a decrease of 1,900 and a decrease of 5.59% year-on-year (Figure 4-23).

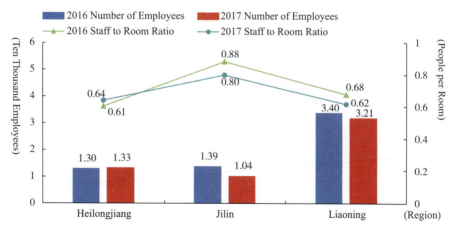

Figure 4-23   The Number of Employees and Staff to Room Ratio of Star-rated Hotels in
Northeast China (2016 and 2017)

In terms of the staff to room ratio of star-rated hotels, there were 0.65 people per room in northeast China in 2017, with a year-on-year decrease of 0.05 people per room and a decrease of 6.50%. Specifically, Heilongjiang had 0.64 people per room, a year-on-year increase of 0.03 people per room, an increase of 4.92%. Jilin was 0.80 people per room, a decrease of 0.08 people per room, and a decrease of 9.09%; Liaoning had 0.62 people per room, a decrease of 0.06 people per room and a decrease of 8.82%.

IV. Analysis of Star-rated Hotel Industry in East China (Shanghai, Jiangsu, Zhejiang, Anhui, Fujian and Shandong)

1. Distribution of Star-rated Hotels by Numbers

In 2017, there were 2,508 star-rated hotels in east China, mainly three star-rated and four star-rated hotels. Specifically, there are 339 five star-rated hotels, accounting for 13.52% of the total star-rated hotels in east China. There are 755 four star-rated hotels, accounting for 30.10% of the total in east China. There are 1,143 three star-rated hotels, accounting for 45.57% of the total in east China. There are 263 two star-rated hotels, accounting for 10.49% of the total in east China. There are 8 one star-rated hotels in total, accounting for 0.32% of the total star-rated hotels in east China (Figure 4-24).

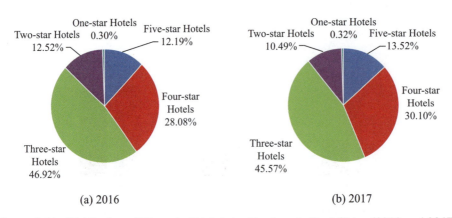

(a) 2016　　　　　　　　　　(b) 2017

Figure 4-24　Distribution of Star-rated Hotels by Numbers in East China (2016 and 2017)

Compared with 2016, the proportion of five star-rated hotels in east China increased by 10.88%, four star-rated hotels increased by 7.22%, three star-rated hotels decreased by 2.86%, two star-rated hotels decreased by 16.26% and one star-rated hotels increased by 7.93%.

In terms of the distribution of star-rated hotels, there were 223 star-rated hotels in Shanghai in 2017, accounting for 8.89% of the star-rated hotels in east China. Jiangsu has 514 star-rated hotels, accounting for 20.49% of the star-rated hotels in east China. There are 585 star-rated hotels in ZheJiang, accounting for 23.33% of the star-rated hotels in east China. There are 294 star-rated hotels in Anhui, accounting for 11.72% of the star-rated hotels in east China. There are 306 starred hotels in Fujian, accounting for 12.20% of the starred hotels in east China. There are 586 star-rated hotels in Shandong, accounting for 23.37% of the total in east China.

Compared with 2016, the number of star-rated hotels in Shanghai, Jiangsu, ZheJiang, Anhui, Fujian and Shandong decreased by 4, 47, 66, 18, 28 and 36, respectively, with the reduction of 1.76%, 8.38%, 10.14%, 5.77%, 8.38% and 5.79% (Figure 4-25).

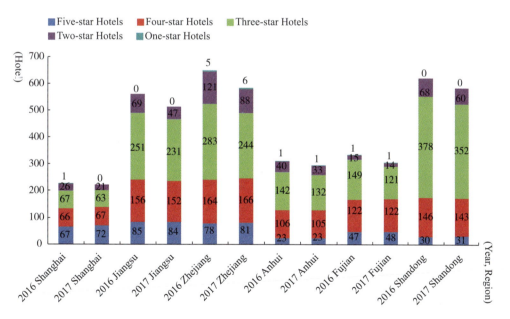

Figure 4-25   Quantity Distribution of Star-rated Hotels with Different Star Grades in East China (2016 and 2017)

In terms of the distribution structure of the number of star-rated hotels, three star-rated hotels dominated in east China in 2017, followed by four-star, two-star, five-star and one star-rated hotels. Specifically, there were 0, 21, 63, 67 and 72 one to five star-rated hotels in Shanghai, accounting for 0%, 9.42%, 28.25%, 30.04% and 32.29%, respectively. There were 0, 47, 231, 152 and 84 one to five star-rated hotels in Jiangsu, accounting for 0%, 9.14%, 44.94%, 29.57% and 16.34%, respectively. There were 6, 88, 244, 166 and 81 one to five star-rated hotels in Zhejiang, accounting for 1.03%, 15.04%, 41.71%, 28.38% and 13.85%, respectively. There were 1, 33, 132, 105 and 23 one to five star-rated hotels in Anhui, accounting for 0.34%, 11.22%, 44.90%, 35.71% and 7.82%, respectively. There were 1, 14, 121, 122 and 48 five star-rated hotels in Fujian, accounting for 0.33%, 4.58%, 39.54%, 39.87% and 15.69% respectively. There were 0, 60, 352, 143 and 31 one to five star-rated hotels in Shandong, accounting for 0%, 10.42%, 60.07%, 24.4% and 5.29% respectively.

2. Distribution of Star-rated Hotels by Revenue

1) Operational Revenue and its Composition

In 2017, the annual operational revenue of star-rated hotels in east China reached 81.456 billion yuan, increasing by 1.92% year-on-year, of which the room revenue was 34.3 billion yuan, accounting for 42.11% of the operational revenue of star-rated hotels in east China. Food and beverage revenue was 36.287 billion yuan, accounting for 44.55% of the operational revenue of star-rated hotels in east China. Other revenue was 10.87 billion yuan, accounting for 13.34% of the operational revenue of star-rated hotels in east China.

In 2017, the operational revenue was 21.265 billion yuan, 16.34 billion yuan, 18.657 billion yuan, 5.116 billion yuan, 8.60 billion yuan and 11.478 billion yuan in Shanghai, Jiangsu, Zhejiang, Anhui, Fujian, Shandong , respectively, accounting for 26.11%, 20.06%, 22.90%, 6.28%, 10.56% and 14.09%, respectively, with Shanghai taking the largest share. Compared with the same period in 2016, the operational revenue of Shanghai, Jiangsu, Anhui and Shandong increased year-on-year, with growth rates of 6.32%, 3.40%, 3.43% and 3.79%, respectively. The operational revenue of Zhejiang and Fujian decreased year-on-year by 4.23% and 0.33% (Figure 4-26).

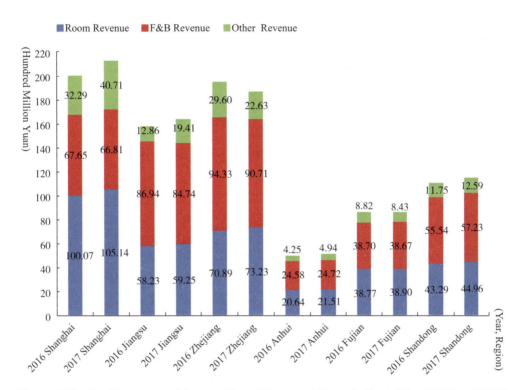

Figure 4-26   The Revenue and Composition of Star-rated Hotels in East China (2016 and 2017)

The operational revenue structure of star-rated hotels in east China in 2017 was mainly dominated by the revenue from rooms and food and beverage, accounting for 86.66% of the total revenue. Specifically, consistent with the performance in 2016, the room revenue of Shanghai and Fujian star-rated hotels exceeded the food and beverage revenue, accounting for 49.44% and 45.24% of the total operational revenue respectively. The food and beverage revenue of Jiangsu, ZheJiang, Anhui and Shandong star-rated hotels exceeded the room revenue, accounting for 51.86, 48.62%, 48.31% and 49.86%, respectively (Table 4-3).

Table 4-3   The Share of Operational Revenues of Star-rated Hotels in East China (2016 and 2017)

	Room Revenue (%)		Food and Beverage Revenue (%)		Other Revenue (%)	
	2016	2017	2016	2017	2016	2017
East China	41.53	42.11	46.01	44.55	12.46	13.34
Shanghai	50.03	49.44	33.83	31.42	16.14	19.14
Jiangsu	36.85	36.26	55.01	51.86	8.14	11.88
Zhejiang	36.39	39.25	48.42	48.62	15.19	12.13
Anhui	41.73	42.04	49.68	48.31	8.59	9.65
Fujian	44.93	45.24	44.85	44.96	10.22	9.80
Shandong	39.15	39.17	50.22	49.86	10.63	10.97

(2) Operational Revenue of Each Hundred-Yuan Fixed Asset

In terms of the operational revenue realized by the each hundred-yuan fixed assets of star-rated hotels, the annual revenue of east China in 2017 was 48.14 yuan, with an increase of 0.93 yuan year-on-year and an increase of 1.97%. Specifically, Shanghai star-rated hotels had the strongest revenue generating capacity in fixed asset investment, which was 65.20 yuan, with an increase of 4.77 yuan year-on-year and an increase of 7.89%. Jiangsu was 45.90 yuan, with a decrease of 0.21 yuan year-on-year and a decrease of 0.46%. Zhejiang was 43.47 yuan, with a decrease of 1.54 yuan year-on-year and a decrease of 3.42%. Anhui was 38.14 yuan, with an increase of 1.31 yuan year-on-year and an increase of 3.56%; Fujian was 57.99 yuan, with a decrease of 1.10 yuan year-on-year and a decrease of 1.86%. Shandong was 38.47 yuan, with an increase of 3.36 yuan year-on-year and an increase of 9.57% (Figure 4-27).

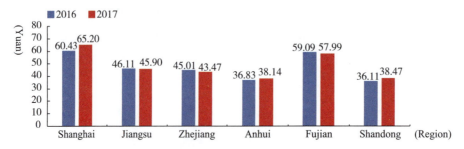

Figure 4-27   Operational Revenues of Each Hundred-yuan Fixed Assets of Star-rated Hotels in East China (2016 and 2017)

(3) Operational Revenues per Room

In terms of the operational revenue per room of the star-rated hotel, the annual revenue of east China in 2017 was 197,100 yuan, up by 9,400 yuan year-on-year, an increase of 5.03%. Specifically, Shanghai reached 362,500 yuan, with an increase of 14,800 yuan year-on-year and an increase of 4.26%. Jiangsu reached 207,200 yuan, with an increase of 15,400 yuan year-on-year and an increase of 8.03%. Zhejiang reached 189,700 yuan, with a decrease of 3,000 yuan year-on-year and a decrease of 1.56%. Anhui reached 119,300 yuan, with an increase of 7,600 yuan year-on-year and an increase of 6.80%. Fujian reached 164,300 yuan, with an increase of 4,400 yuan year-on-year and an increase of 2.75%. Shandong reached 139,800 yuan, with an increase of 12,000 yuan year-on-year and an increase of 9.39% (Figure 4-28).

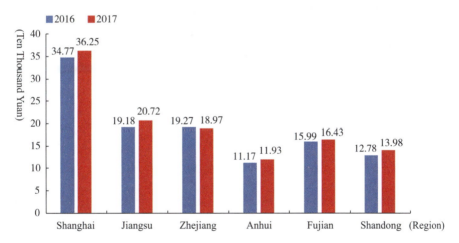

Figure 4-28   Operational Revenues of Each Room of Star-rated Hotels in East China (2016 and 2017)

(4) Fixed Assets for Each Hundred-yuan Operational Revenue

In terms of the fixed assets occupied by each hundred-yuan of operational revenue of star-rated hotels, the annual revenue of east China was 207.74 yuan in 2017, which decreased by 4.10 yuan year-on-year and decreased by 1.93%. Specifically, Shanghai reached 153.37 yuan, with a decrease of 12.12 yuan year-on-year and a decrease of 7.32%. Jiangsu reached 217.87 yuan, with an increase of 1.02 yuan year-on-year and an increase of 0.47%. Zhejiang reached 230.06 yuan, with an increase of 7.89 yuan year-on-year and an increase of 3.55%. Anhui reached 262.20 yuan, with a decrease of 46.35 yuan year-on-year and a decrease of 3.43%. Fujian reached 172.45 yuan, with an increase of 3.20 yuan year-on-year and an increase of 1.89%; Shandong reached 259.96 yuan, with a decrease of 16.93 yuan, a year-on-year decrease of 16.93 yuan and a decrease of 6.11% (Figure 4-29).

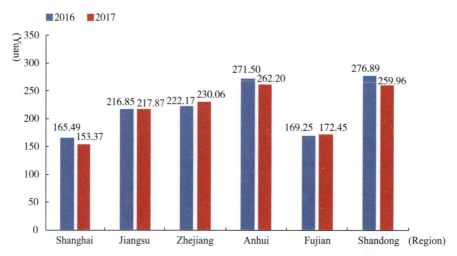

Figure 4-29   Fix Assets for Each Hundred-Yuan Operational Revenues of Star-rated Hotels in East China (2016 and 2017)

3. Distribution of Star-rated Hotels by Total Profit

In terms of the total profits of star-rated hotels, the annual profit of east China in 2017 was 4.885 billion yuan, up 2.765 billion yuan year-on-year, increasing by 130.36%. Specifically, only Shandong lost money in 2017, and all other regions achieved profits. The total profit in Shanghai was 3.345 billion yuan, and the year-on-year profit increased by 396 million yuan, an increase of 13.43%. Jiangsu earned 529 million yuan, and its year-on-year profit increased by 699 million yuan, an increase of 411.18%. Zhejiang earned 803 million yuan, with a year-on-year profit increase of 1.078 billion yuan, an increase of 392%. Anhui earned 90 million yuan, up 122 million yuan from a year earlier, an increase of 381.25%. The profit in Fujian was 337 million yuan, the year-on-year profit increased by 150 million yuan, the increase was 80.21%. Shandong lost 218 million yuan, and its year-on-year profit increased by 321 million yuan, an increase of 59.55% (Figure 4-30).

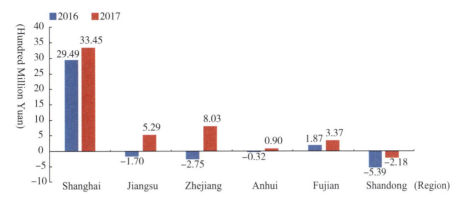

Figure 4-30   Total Profits of Star-rated Hotels in East China (2016 and 2017)

4. Distribution of Star-rated Hotels by Human Resources

In terms of the number of star-rated hotel employees, 367,100 were employed in east China in 2017, with a decrease of 28,400 year-on-year and a decrease of 7.17%. Specifically, Shanghai was 50,800, with a decrease of 2,200 year-on-year and a decrease of 4.15%. Jiangsu was 74,500, with a decrease of 5,500 year-on-year and a decrease of 6.88%. ZheJiang was 87,600, with a decrease of 7,500 year-on-year and a decrease of 7.89%. Anhui was 33,100, with a decrease of 1,400 year-on-year and a decrease of 4.06%. Fujian was 48,500 people, with a decrease of 5,000 year-on-year and a decrease of 9.35%. Shandong was 72,700, with a decrease of 6,700 year-on-year and a decrease of 8.44% (Figure 4-31).

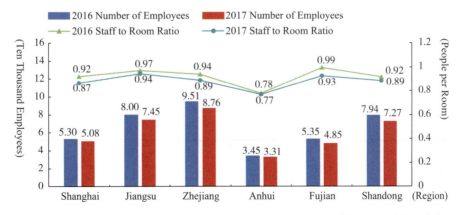

Figure 4-31   The Number of Employees and Staff to Room Ratio of Star-rated Hotels in East China (2016 and 2017)

In terms of the staff to room ratio of star-rated hotels, the number of people in east China in 2017 was 0.89 people per room, with a decrease of 0.04 people per room and a decrease of 4.34% year-on-year. Specifically, Shanghai was 0.87 people per room, with a decrease of 0.05 people per room and a decrease of 5.43% year-on-year. Jiangsu was 0.94 people per room, with a decrease of 0.03 people per room and a decrease of 3.09% year-on-year. Zhejiang was 0.89 people per room, with a decrease of 0.05 people per room and a decrease of 5.32% year-on-year. In Anhui province, there were 0.77 people per room, with a decrease of 0.01 people per room and a decrease of 1.28% year-on-year. Fujian was 0.93 people per room, with a decrease of 0.06 people per room and a decrease of 6.06% year-on-year. Shandong was 0.89 people per room, with a decrease of 0.03 people per room and a decrease of 3.26% year-on-year.

V. Analysis of Star-rated Hotel Industry in South China (Guangdong, Guangxi and Hainan)

1. Distribution of Star-rated Hotels by Numbers

In 2017, there were 1,148 star-rated hotels in south China, mainly three star-rated and four star-rated hotels. Specifically, there are 136 five star-rated hotels, accounting for 11.85% of the total star-level hotels in south China. There are 260 four star-rated hotels, accounting for 22.65% of the total in south China. There are 622 three star-rated hotels, accounting for 54.18% of the total in south China. There are 126 two star-rated hotels, accounting for 10.98% of the total in south China. There are 4 one star-rated hotels in total, accounting for 0.35% of the total star-rated hotels in south China (Figure 4-32).

Compared with 2016, the proportion of five star-rated hotels increased by 4.13%, four star-rated hotels increased by 6.62%, three star-rated hotels decreased by 0.72%, two star-rated hotels decreased by 11.56%, and one-star hotels decreased by 12.40%.

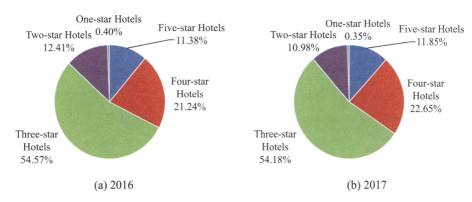

(a) 2016   (b) 2017

Figure 4-32   Distribution of Star-rated Hotels by Numbers in South China (2016 and 2017)

According to the distribution of star-rated hotels, there were 658 star-rated hotels in Guangdong in 2017, accounting for 57.32% of the star-rated hotels in south China. There are 370 star-rated hotels in Guangxi, accounting for 32.23% of that in south China. There are 120 star-rated hotels in Hainan, accounting for 10.45% of the star-rated hotels in south China.

Compared with 2016, the number of star-rated hotels in Guangdong, Guangxi and Hainan decreased by 65, 40 and 4, respectively, with a decrease of 8.99%, 9.76% and 3.23% (Figure 4-33).

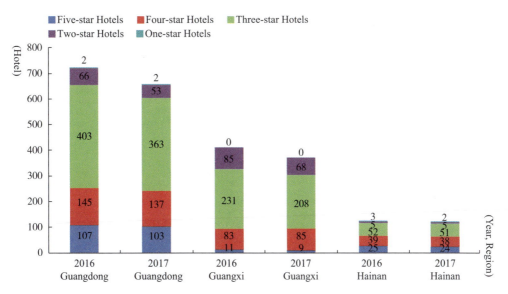

Figure 4-33   Quantity Distribution of Star-rated Hotels with Different Star Grades in South China (2016 and 2017)

In terms of the distribution structure of the number of star-rated hotels, three star-rated hotels dominated in south China in 2017, followed by four-star, five-star, two-star and one star-rated hotels. Specifically, there are 2, 53, 363, 137 and 103 one to five star-rated hotels in Guangdong, accounting for 0.30%, 8.05%, 55.17%, 20.82% and 15.65% of the total hotels in Guangdong. There are 0, 68, 208, 85 and 9 one to five star-rated hotels in Guangxi, accounting for 0%, 18.38%, 56.22%, 22.97% and 2.43% respectively of the total hotels in Guangxi. There are 2, 5, 51, 38 and 24 one to five star-rated hotels in Hainan, accounting for 1.67%, 4.17%, 42.50%, 31.67% and 20.00% respectively of the total hotels in Hainan.

2. Distribution of Star-rated Hotels by Revenue

(1) Operational Revenue and its Composition

In 2017, the annual operational revenue of star-rated hotels in south China reached 29.401 billion yuan, a year-on-year decrease of 0.22%, of which the room revenue reached 14.089 billion yuan, accounting for 47.92% of the operational revenue of star-rated hotels in south China. Food and beverage revenue reached 11.11 billion yuan, accounting for 37.79% of the operational revenue of star-rated hotels in south China; Other revenue reached 4.202 billion yuan, accounting for 14.29% of the operational revenue of star-rated hotels in south China.

In south China in 2017, Guangdong, Guangxi and Hainan accounted for 21.083 billion yuan, 3.776 billion yuan and 4.542 billion yuan, respectively, accounting for 71.71%, 12.84% and 15.45%, with Guangdong taking the largest share. Compared with 2016, the operational revenue of Guangdong and Guangxi decreased year on year, with a decrease of 0.17% and 4.46%, respectively. Hainan's operational revenue increased year-on-year, with an increase of 3.39% (Figure 4-34).

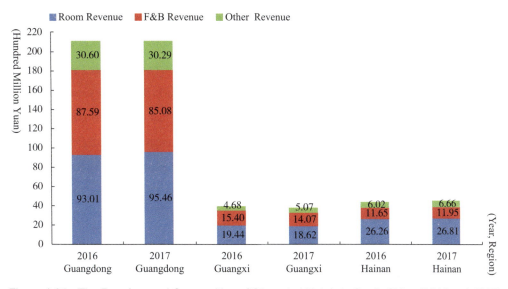

Figure 4-34   The Revenue and Composition of Star-rated Hotels in South China (2016 and 2017)

In 2017, the operational revenue structure of star-rated hotels in south China is mainly dominated by the revenue from rooms and food and beverage, accounting for 85.71% of the total revenue. To be specific, consistent with the performance in 2016, the revenue gap between hotel rooms and food and beverage in Guangxi and Hainan is large, which is dominated by the room revenue. The proportion of room revenue in the total operational revenue is 49.32% and 59.02%, respectively. The revenue of rooms and food and beverage in Guangdong is equalent, accounting for 45.28% and 40.35% respectively (Table 4-4).

Table 4-4   The Share of Operational Revenues of Star-rated Hotels in South China (2016 and 2017)

	Room Revenue (%)		Food and Beverage Revenue (%)		Other Revenue (%)	
	2016	2017	2016	2017	2016	2017
South China	47.08	47.92	38.90	37.79	14.02	14.29
Guangdong	44.04	45.28	41.47	40.35	14.49	14.37
Guangxi	49.19	49.32	38.96	37.25	11.85	13.43
Hainan	59.79	59.02	26.51	26.32	13.70	14.66

(2) Operational Revenue of Each Hundred-Yuan Fixed Asset

In terms of the operational revenue of each hundred-yuan fixed assets of star-rated hotels, the annual revenue in 2017 in south China was 45.83 yuan, with a year-on-year increase of 7.88 yuan and an increase of 20.76%. To be specific, Guangdong star-rated hotels had the strongest revenue generating capacity in fixed asset investment, which was 48.90 yuan, with an increase of 11.54 yuan year-on-year and an increase of 30.89%. Guangxi reported 42.05 yuan, with an increase of 1.71 yuan year-on-year and an increase of 4.24%. Hainan reached 37.67 yuan, with a decrease of 1.20 yuan year-on-year and a decrease of 3.09% (Figure 4-35).

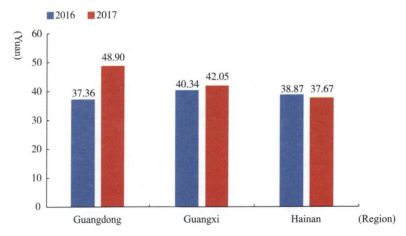

Figure 4-35   Operational Revenues of Each Hundred-yuan Fixed Assets of Star-rated Hotels in South China (2016 and 2017)

(3) Operational Revenues per Room

In terms of the operational revenue per room of the star-rated hotel, the annual revenue of south China was 154,600 yuan in 2017, with an increase of 8,000 yuan year-on-year and an increase of 5.47%. Specifically, Guangdong reached 181,600 yuan, with an increase of 7,700 yuan year-on-year and an increase of 4.43%. Guangxi reached 77,900 yuan, with an increase of 2,800 yuan year-on-year and an increase of 3.73%. Hainan reached 177,700 yuan, with an increase of 14,400 yuan year-on-year and an increase of 8.82% (Figure 4-36).

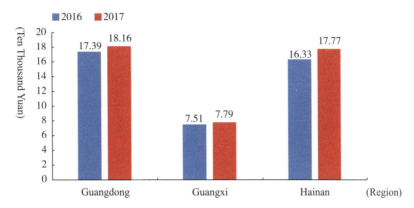

Figure 4-36   Operational Revenues of Each Room of Star-rated Hotels in South China (2016 and 2017)

(4) Fixed Assets for Each Hundred-yuan Operational Revenue

In terms of the each hundred-yuan operational revenue of star-rated hotels, the fixed assets were occupied by 218.19 yuan in south China in 2017, down by 45.29 yuan year-on-year, down by 17.19%. Specifically, Guangdong was 204.49 yuan, a year-on-year decrease of 63.19 yuan, a decrease of 23.61%; Guangxi was 237.82 yuan, reduced by 10.09 yuan and 4.07%. Hainan was 265.49 yuan, up 8.25 yuan year-on-year, up 3.21% (Figure 4-37).

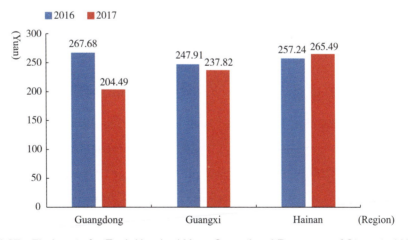

Figure 4-37   Fix Assets for Each Hundred-Yuan Operational Revenues of Star-rated Hotels in South China (2016 and 2017)

3. Distribution of Star-rated Hotels by Total Profit

In terms of the total profit of star-rated hotels, the annual profit of south China in 2017 was 2.507 billion yuan, up 526 million yuan year-on-year, with an increase of 26.55%. Specifically, Guangdong and Hainan were profitable, while Guangxi was losing profits. Guangdong posted a total profit of 2.241 billion yuan, with a year-on-year profit increase of 981 million yuan or 77.86%. Guangxi lost 79 million yuan, a year-on-year loss of 385 million yuan, an increase of loss of 125.82%. Hainan posted a total profit of 346 million yuan, a year-on-year profit decrease of 70 million yuan, a decrease of 16.83% (Figure 4-38).

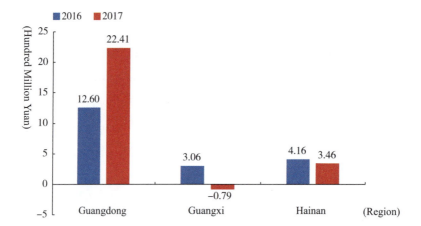

Figure 4-38　Total Profits of Star-rated Hotels in South China (2016 and 2017)

4. Distribution of Star-rated Hotels by Human Resources

In terms of the number of star-rated hotel employees, there were 155,100 in south China in 2017, a year-on-year decrease of 21,300 and a decrease of 12.10%. Specifically, Guangdong was 104,200, with a decrease of 18,700 year-on-year and a decrease of 15.22%. Guangxi was 30,300, with a decrease of 2,300 year-on-year and a decrease of 7.06%. Hainan was 20,600, with a decrease of 400 year-on-year and a decrease of 1.90% (Figure 4-39).

In terms of the staff to room ratio of star-rated hotels, there were 0.82 people per room in south China in 2017, a decrease of 0.06 people per room and a decrease of 7.09%.

Specifically, Guangdong had 0.90 people per room, a decrease of 0.11 people per room, a decrease of 10.89%. Guangxi had 0.62 people per room, unchanged from 2016. Hainan was 0.81 people per room, an increase of 0.03 people per room year on year, an increase of 3.85%.

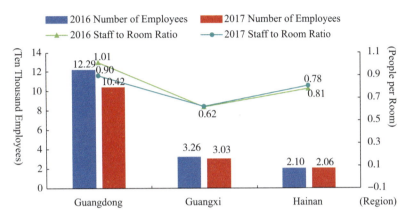

Figure 4-39   The Number of Employees and Staff to Room Ratio of Star-rated Hotels in South China (2010 and 2017)

VI. Analysis of Star-rated Hotel Industry in Central China (Jiangxi, Henan, Hubei and Hunan)

1. Distribution of Star-rated Hotels by Numbers

In 2017, there were 1400 star-rated hotels in central China, mainly including three star-rated and four star-rated hotels. Specifically, there are 74 five star-rated hotels, accounting for 5.29% of the total star-rated hotels in central China. There are 335 four star-rated hotels, accounting for 23.93% of the total in central China. There are 741 three star-rated hotels in total, accounting for 52.93% of the total five star-rated hotels in central China. There are 245 two star-rated hotels, accounting for 17.50% of the total in central China. There are 5 one star-rated hotels in total, accounting for 0.36% of the total star-rated hotels in central China (Figure 4-40).

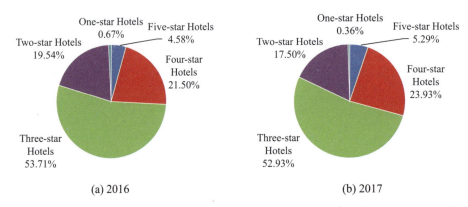

(a) 2016   (b) 2017

Figure 4-40   Distribution of Star-rated Hotels by Numbers in Central China (2016 and 2017)

Compared with 2016, the proportion of five star-rated hotels in central China increased by 15.35%, four star-rated hotels increased by 11.32%, three star-rated hotels decreased by 1.45%, two star-rated hotels decreased by 10.45% and one star-rated hotels decreased by 47.00%.

In terms of the distribution of star-rated hotels, there were 281 star-rated hotels in Jiangxi in 2017, accounting for 20.07% of the star-rated hotels in central China. There are 389 star-rated hotels in Henan, accounting for 27.79% of the star-rated hotels in central China. There are 364 star-rated hotels in Hubei, accounting for 26% of the number in central China. There are 366 star-rated hotels in Hunan, accounting for 26.14% of the number in central China.

Compared with 2016, the number of star rated hotels in Jiangxi, Henan and Hunan decreased by 9, 22 and 53, respectively, with a decrease of 3.10%, 5.35% and 12.65%, respectively. The number of star-rated hotels in Hubei remains unchanged (Figure 4-41).

In terms of the distribution structure of the number of star-rated hotels, three star-rated hotels dominated in central China in 2017, followed by four-star, two-star, five-star and one star-rated hotels. Specifically, there are 0, 19, 149, 100 and 13 one to five star-rated hotels in Jiangxi, accounting for 0%, 6.76%, 53.02%, 35.59% and 4.63% respectively. There are 1, 55, 231, 83 and 19 one star-rated to five star-rated hotels in Henan, accounting for 0.26%, 14.14%, 59.38%, 21.34% and 4.88% respectively. There are 4, 86, 166, 85 and 23 one star-rated to five star-rated hotels in Hubei, accounting for 1.10%, 23.63%, 45.60%,

23.35% and 6.32% of total hotels in Hubei. The number of one star-rated to five star-rated hotels in Hunan is 0, 85, 195, 67 and 19 respectively, accounting for 0%, 23.22%, 53.28%, 18.31% and 5.19% respectively.

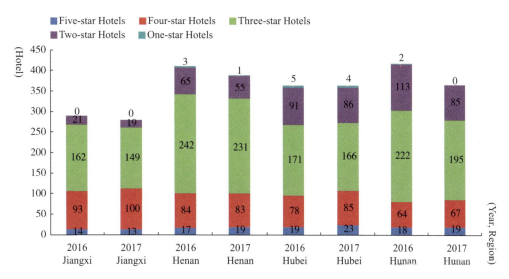

Figure 4-41   Quantity Distribution of Star-rated Hotels with Different Star Grades in Central China (2016 and 2017)

2. Distribution of Star-rated Hotels by Revenue

(1) Operational Revenue and its Composition

In 2017, the operational revenue of star-rated hotels in central China reached 20.318 billion yuan, up 1.28% year-on-year, of which the room revenue was 9.317 billion yuan, accounting for 45.85% of the operational revenue of star-rated hotels in central China. Food and beverage revenue was 8.798 billion yuan, accounting for 43.30% of the operational revenue of star-rated hotels in central China. Other revenue was 2.203 billion yuan, accounting for 10.84% of the operational revenue of star-rated hotels in central China.

In central China in 2017, the operational revenue of Jiangxi, Henan, Hubei and Hunan was 3.302 billion yuan, 5.766 billion yuan, 5.213 billion yuan and 6.036 billion yuan, respectively, accounting for 16.25%, 28.38%, 25.66% and 29.71%, with Hunan taking the largest share. Compared with 2016, the operational revenue of Jiangxi and Hunan decreased year on year, with a decrease of 3.15% and 4.27%, respectively. The operational revenue of Henan and Hubei increased by 2.62% and 10.28%, respectively (Figure 4-42).

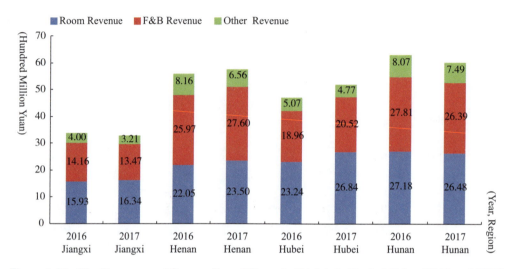

Figure 4-42   The Revenue and Composition of Star-rated Hotels in Central China (2016 and 2017)

The operational revenue structure of star-rated hotels in central China in 2017 is mainly dominated by room and food and beverage revenue, accounting for 89.15% of total revenue. Specifically, consistent with the performance in 2016, the room revenue of Jiangxi star-rated hotels exceeded the revenue of food and beverage, accounting for 49.49% and 40.80% of the total operational revenue respectively. The food and beverage revenue of star-rated hotels in Henan exceeded the room revenue, accounting for 47.87% and 40.76%, respectively. There is a large gap between the revenue of hotel rooms and food and beverage in Hubei, accounting for 51.48% and 39.37% of the total operational revenue respectively. The revenue of hotel rooms and food and beverage in Hunan is equalent, accounting for 43.87% and 43.71% of the total operational revenue respectively (Table 4-5).

Table 4-5   The Share of Operational Revenues of Star-rated Hotels in Central China (2016 and 2017)

	Room Revenue (%)		Food and Beverage Revenue (%)		Other Revenue (%)	
	2016	2017	2016	2017	2016	2017
Central China	44.07	45.85	43.32	43.30	12.61	10.84
Jiangxi	46.74	49.49	41.53	40.80	11.73	9.71
Henan	39.25	40.76	46.22	47.87	14.53	11.37
Hubei	49.16	51.48	40.10	39.37	10.73	9.15
Hunan	43.10	43.87	44.11	43.71	12.79	12.42

(2) Operational Revenue of Each Hundred-Yuan Fixed Asset

In terms of the each hundred-yuan fixed assets realized by star-rated hotels, the revenue in central China in 2017 was 42.09 yuan, up 1.64 yuan year-on-year, with an increase of 4.06%. Specifically, Jiangxi star-rated hotel's fixed asset investment has the strongest earning capacity, which is 45.58 yuan, up 2.95 yuan year-on-year, with an increase of 6.92%. Henan was 43.43 yuan, up 1.55 yuan year-on-year, an increase of 3.70%. Hubei was 41.62 yuan, a year-on-year increase of 3.13 yuan, an increase of 8.13%; Hunan was 39.65 yuan, unchanged from 2016 (Figure 4-43).

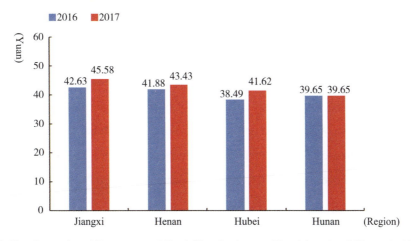

Figure 4-43   Operational Revenues of Each Hundred-yuan Fixed Assets of Star-rated Hotels in Central China (2016 and 2017)

(3) Operational Revenues per Room

In terms of the operational revenue per room of star-rated hotels, the operational revenue per room in central China in 2017 was 107,100 yuan, up 3,600 yuan year-on-year, an increase of 3.48%. Specifically, Jiangxi was 85,100 yuan, with a decrease of 1,000 yuan and a decrease of 1.16%. Henan was 109,500 yuan, an increase of 5,300 yuan or 5.09% year-on-year. Hubei was 107,300 yuan, up 7,400 yuan year-on-year, up 7.41%. Hunan increased by 2,500 yuan and increased by 2.10% year-on-year (Figure 4-44).

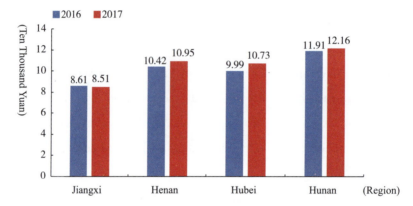

Figure 4-44   Operational Revenues of Each Room of Star-rated Hotels in Central China (2016 and 2017)

(4) Fixed Assets for Each Hundred-yuan Operational Revenue

In terms of the fixed assets occupied by each hundred-yuan of operational revenue of star-rated hotels, the central China in 2017 reached 237.59 yuan, a year-on-year decrease of 9.64 yuan and a decrease of 3.90%. Specifically, Jiangxi reached 219.41 yuan, a year-on-year decrease of 15.15 yuan and a decrease of 6.46%. Henan reached 230.26 yuan, a year-on-year decrease of 8.53 yuan and a decrease of 3.57%. Hubei reached 240.29 yuan, a year-on-year decrease of 19.49 yuan and a decrease of 7.50%. Hunan reached 252.20 yuan, a year-on-year decrease of 0.01 yuan and a decrease of 0.004% (Figure 4-45).

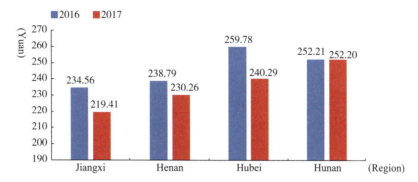

Figure 4-45   Fix Assets for Each Hundred-Yuan Operational Revenues of Star-rated Hotels in

Central China (2016 and 2017)

3. Distribution of Star-rated Hotels by Total Profit

In terms of the total profit of star-rated hotels, the annual profit in central China in 2017 was 346 million yuan, up by 2.946 billion yuan year-on-year, up by 113.31%. In particular, Jiangxi, Hubei and Hunan were profitable, while Henan was in the red. Jiangxi's total profit was 91 million yuan, while its year-on-year profit increased by 32 million yuan, increasing by 54.24%. Henan lost 195 million yuan, a decrease of loss of 715 million yuan year-on-year, down 78.57%. The total profit of Hubei was 74 million yuan, and the year-on-year profit increased by 1.757 billion yuan, increasing by 104.40%. Hunan's total profit was 376 million yuan, up 442 million yuan year-on-year, up 669.70% (Figure 4-46).

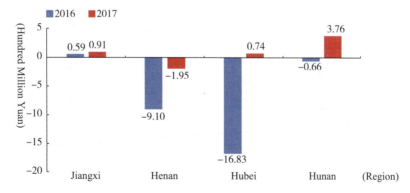

Figure 4-46 Total Profits of Star-rated Hotels in Central China (2016 and 2017)

4. Distribution of Star-rated Hotels by Human Resources

The number of star-rated hotel employees in central China was 144,800 in 2017, down 7,900 year-on-year, a decrease of 5.17%. Specifically, Jiangxi was 24,800, with a year-on-year decrease of 1,500 and a decrease of 5.70%. Henan was 42,200, with a year-on-year decrease of 3,500 and a decrease of 7.66%. Hubei was 36,300 people, with a year-on-year increase of 1,700 and an increase of 4.91%. Hunan was 41,400, with a year-on-year decrease of 4,800 and a decrease of 10.39% (Figure 4-47).

In terms of the staff to room ratio of star-rated hotels, there were 0.76 people per room in central China in 2017, a decrease of 0.02 people per room year on year, a decrease of 3.11%. Specifically, Jiangxi was 0.64 people per room, with a year-on-year decrease of 0.03 people per room, a decrease of 4.48%. Henan was 0.80 people per room, with a year-on-year decrease of 0.05 people per room and a decrease of 5.88%. Hubei was 0.75 people per room, with a year-on-year increase of 0.02 people per room, an increase of 2.74%. Hunan was 0.84 people per room, with a year-on-year decrease of 0.03 people per room, a decrease of 3.45%.

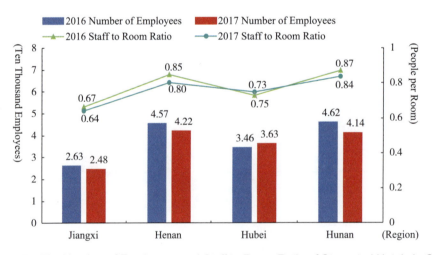

Figure 4-47   The Number of Employees and Staff to Room Ratio of Star-rated Hotels in Central China (2016 and 2017)

VII. Analysis of Star-rated Hotel Industry in Southwest China (Chongqing, Sichuan, Guizhou, Yunnan and Tibet)

1. Distribution of Star-rated Hotels by Numbers

In 2017, there were 1,331 star-rated hotels in southwest China, mainly including three star-rated and four star-rated hotels. Specifically, there are 80 five star-rated hotels, accounting for 6.01% of the total star-rated hotels in southwest China. There are 313 four star-rated hotels in total, accounting for 23.52% of the total star-rated hotels in southwest China. There are 533 three star-rated hotels, accounting for 40.05% of the total star-level hotels in southwest China. There are 377 two star-rated hotels, accounting for 28.32% of the total in southwest China. There are 28 one star-rated hotels in total, accounting for 2.10% of the total star-rated hotels in southwest China (figure 4-48).

Compared with 2016, the proportion of five star-rated hotels in southwest China increased by 12.74%, four star-rated hotels by 15.75%, three star-rated hotels by 1.80%, two star-rated hotels by 7.93% and one star-rated hotels by 25.13%.

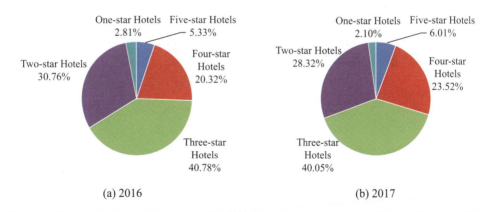

(a) 2016   (b) 2017

Figure 4-48   Distribution of Star-rated Hotels by Numbers in Southwest China (2016 and 2017)

According to the distribution of star-rated hotels, there were 188 star-rated hotels in Chongqing in 2017, accounting for 14.12% of the star-rated hotels in southwest China.

There are 323 star-rated hotels in Sichuan, accounting for 24.27% of the total in southwest China. Guizhou has 232 star-rated hotels, accounting for 17.43% of the number of star-rated hotels in southwest China. There are 518 star-rated hotels in Yunnan, accounting for 38.92% of the star-rated hotels in southwest China. There are 70 star-rated hotels in Tibet, accounting for 5.26% of the total in southwest China.

Compared with 2016, the number of star-rated hotels in Chongqing, Guizhou and Yunnan decreased by 9, 34 and 41, respectively, with a decrease of 4.57%, 12.78% and 7.33%, respectively. The number of star-rated hotels in Sichuan and Tibet increased by 25 and 2, respectively, by 8.39% and 2.94% year-on-year (Figure 4-49).

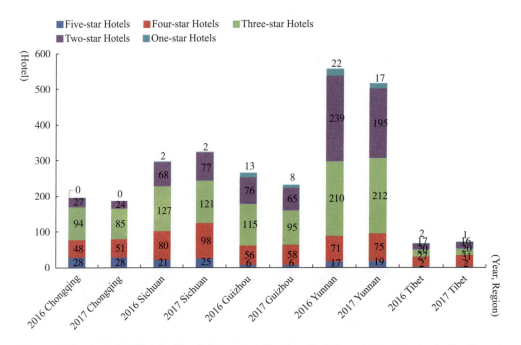

Figure 4-49   Quantity Distribution of Star-rated Hotels with Different Star Grades in Southwest China (2016 and 2017)

According to the distribution structure of the number of star-rated hotels, three star-rated hotels dominated the southwest China in 2017, followed by two-star, four-star, five-star and one star-rated hotels. Specifically, the number of one star-rated to five star-rated hotels in Chongqing is 0, 24, 85, 51 and 28 respectively, accounting for 0%, 12.77%,

45.21%, 27.13% and 14.89%, respectively. There are 2, 77, 121, 98 and 25 one star-rated to five star-rated hotels in Sichuan, accounting for 0.62%, 23.84%, 37.46%, 30.34% and 7.74% respectively. There are 8,65,95,58 and 6 one to five star-rated hotels in Guizhou, accounting for 3.45%, 28.02%, 40.95%, 25.00% and 2.59%, respectively. There are 17, 195, 212, 75 and 19 one star-rated to five star-rated hotels in Yunnan, accounting for 3.28%, 37.64%, 40.93%, 14.48% and 3.67% respectively. There are 1, 16, 20, 31 and 2 one star-rated to five star-rated hotels in Tibet, accounting for 1.43%, 22.86%, 28.57%, 44.29% and 2.86% respectively.

2. Distribution of Star-rated Hotels by Revenue

(1) Operational Revenue and its Composition

In 2017, the annual operational revenue of star-rated hotels in southwest China reached 17.525 billion yuan, an increase of 6.00% year-on-year, including 8.701 billion yuan in room revenue, accounting for 49.65% of the operational revenue of star-rated hotels in southwest China. Food and beverage revenue was 6.04 billion yuan, accounting for 34.46% of the operational revenue of star-rated hotels in southwest China. Other revenue was 2.784 billion yuan, accounting for 15.89% of the operational revenue of star-rated hotels in southwest China.

In southwest China in 2017, the operational revenue of Chongqing, Sichuan, Guizhou, Yunnan and Tibet was 3.734 billion yuan, 6.196 billion yuan, 2.616 billion yuan, 3.919 billion yuan and 1.058 billion yuan, respectively, accounting for 21.31%, 35.36%, 14.93%, 22.36% and 6.04%, respectively, with Sichuan taking the largest share. Compared with the same period in 2016, the operational revenue of Sichuan, Guizhou, Yunnan and Tibet increased by 11.16%, 1.99%, 5.46% and 89.81%, respectively. The operational revenue of Chongqing decreased year-on-year by 9.33% (Figure 4-50).

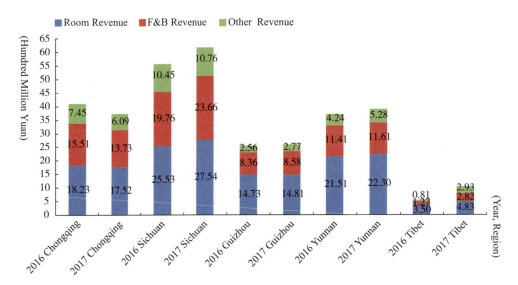

Figure 4-50   The Revenue and Composition of Star-rated Hotels in Southwest

China (2016 and 2017)

The operational revenue structure of star-rated hotels in southwest China in 2017 is mainly dominated by the revenue from rooms and food and beverage, accounting for 84.11% of the total revenue. Specifically, consistent with the performance in 2016, the room revenue in Chongqing, Sichuan, Guizhou, Yunnan and Tibet star-rated hotels exceeded the food and beverage revenue, accounting for 46.92%, 44.45%, 56.60%, 56.91% and 45.66% of the total operational revenue respectively (Table 4-6).

Table 4-6   The Share of Operational Revenues of Star-rated Hotels in Southwest China (2016 and 2017)

	Room Revenue (%)		Food and Beverage Revenue (%)		Other Revenue (%)	
	2016	2017	2016	2017	2016	2017
Southwest China	50.50	49.65	34.06	34.46	15.43	15.89
Chongqing	44.27	46.92	37.65	36.77	18.08	16.31
Sichuan	45.80	44.45	35.45	38.18	18.76	17.37
Guizhou	57.40	56.60	32.61	32.80	9.99	10.61
Yunnan	57.89	56.91	30.70	29.61	11.42	13.47
Tibet	62.69	45.66	22.85	26.66	14.46	27.68

(2) Operational Revenue of Each Hundred-Yuan Fixed Asset

In terms of the each hundred-yuan fixed assets realized by star-rated hotels, the southwest region in 2017 reached 32.76 yuan, with a year-on-year increase of 0.40 yuan, an increase of 1.24%. Specifically, the investment in fixed assets of Guizhou star-rated hotels has the strongest earning capacity, which was 49.60 yuan, with a year-on-year increase of 8.10 yuan, an increase of 19.52%. Chongqing reached 41.46 yuan, with a year-on-year decrease of 1.95 yuan, a decrease of 4.49%. Sichuan reached 35.44 yuan, with a year-on-year increase of 0.11 yuan, an increase of 0.31%. Yunnan reached 23.05 yuan, with a year-on-year increase of 0.16 yuan, an increase of 0.70%. Tibet reached 22.38 yuan, with a year-on-year increase of 6.05 yuan, an increase of 37.05% (Figure 4-51).

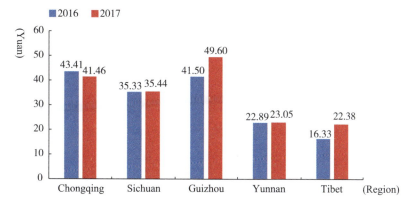

Figure 4-51   Operational Revenues of Each Hundred-yuan Fixed Assets of Star-rated Hotels in Southwest China (2016 and 2017)

(3) Operational Revenues per Room

In terms of the operational revenue per room of the star-rated hotel, the southwest region in 2017 reached 106,000 yuan, with a year-on-year increase of 5,200 yuan, an increase of 5.20%. Specifically, Chongqing reached 134,800 yuan, with a year-on-year decrease of 8,400 yuan, a decrease of 5.87%. Sichuan reached 131,400 yuan, with a year-on-year increase of 4,100 yuan, an increase of 3.22%. Guizhou reached 98,100 yuan, with a year-on-year increase of 6,600 yuan, an increase of 7.21%. Yunnan reached 70,800 yuan, with an increase of 5,200 yuan and an increase of 7.93%. Tibet reached 126,400 yuan, an increase of 44,500 yuan, an increase of 54.33% (Figure 4-52).

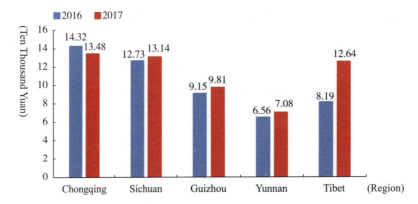

Figure 4-52　Operational Revenues of Each Room of Star-rated Hotels in Southwest China (2016 and 2017)

(4) Operational Revenues of Each Hundred-yuan Fixed Assets

According to the fixed assets occupied by each hundred-yuan of operational revenue of star-rated hotels, the southwest region in 2017 was 305.28 yuan, which decreased by 3.79 yuan year-on-year, with a decrease of 1.23%. Specifically, Chongqing was 241.18 yuan, up 10.82 yuan and 4.70% year-on-year. Sichuan was 282.17 yuan, down 0.84 yuan and 0.30%. Guizhou was 201.61 yuan, a year-on-year decrease of 39.33 yuan and a decrease of 16.32%. Yunnan was 433.90 yuan, a year-on-year decrease of 3.03 yuan, a decrease of 0.69%. Tibet was 446.74 yuan, a decrease of 165.61 yuan and a decrease of 27.04% (Figure 4-53).

Figure 4-53　Fix Assets for Each Hundred-Yuan Operational Revenues of Star-rated Hotels in Southwest China (2016 and 2017)

3. Distribution of Star-rated Hotels by Total Profit

The annual profit of southwest China in 2017 was 26 million yuan, with a year-on-year increase of 280 million yuan , an increase of 110.27% from the total profit of star-rated hotels. To be specific, only Guizhou has been profitable for two years, while other regions are in deficit. The loss in Chongqing was 22 million yuan, and the year-on-year loss was reduced by 44 million yuan to 66.67%. Sichuan lost 54 million yuan, and the year-on-year loss was reduced by 246 million yuan to 82.00%; The total profit of Guizhou was 163 million yuan, the year-on-year profit increased by 65 million yuan, the increase was 66.33%. Yunnan lost 26 million yuan, a year-on-year increase of 42 million yuan, an increase of loss of 262.50%. The loss in Tibet was 35 million yuan, with a year-on-year increase of 34 million yuan, an increase of loss of 340.00% (Figure 4-54).

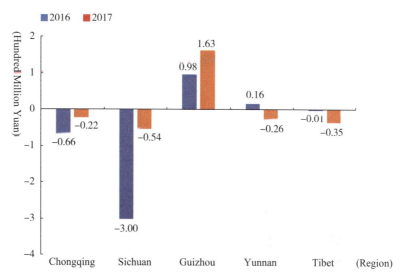

Figure 4-54   Total Profits of Star-rated Hotels in Southwest China (2016 and 2017)

4. Distribution of Star-rated Hotels by Human Resources

In terms of the number of star-rated hotel employees, in the southwest China, the number was 126,000 in 2017, with a decrease of 6,200 and a decrease of 4.70% year-on-year. Specifically, Chongqing was 22,600, down 5,900 and 20.70%. In Sichuan province, there were 40,400 people, an increase of 2,600 and an increase of 6.88%. Guizhou witnessed a decrease of 0.18 million and a decrease of 9.63%. In Yunnan province, there were 41,600 people, 1,800 less than that of the previous year, with a decrease of 4.15%. Tibet was 4,600, an increase of 700, an increase of 17.95% (figure 4-55).

In terms of the staff to room ratio of star-rated hotels, the southwest region was 0.76 people per room in 2017, with a decrease of 0.04 people per room year-on-year, with a decrease of 5.42%. Specifically, Chongqing was 0.81 people per room, with a decrease of 0.18 people per room year on year, with a decrease of 18.18%. Sichuan was 0.86 people per room, unchanged from 2016. Guizhou was 0.64 people per room, with a decrease of 0.03 people per room year on year, with a decrease of 4.48%. There were 0.75 people per room in Yunnan, with a decrease of 0.02 people per room year on year, with a decrease of 2.60%. Tibet was 0.54 people per room, with a decrease of 0.03 people per room year on year, with a decrease of 5.26%.

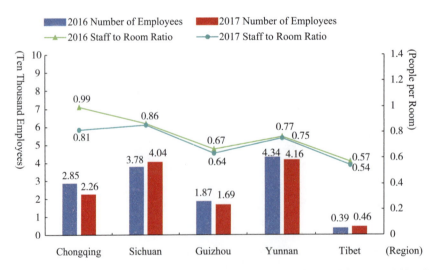

Figure 4-55　The Number of Employees and Staff to Room Ratio of Star-rated Hotels in Southwest China (2016 and 2017)

VIII. Analysis of Star-rated Hotel Industry in Northwest China (Shaanxi, Gansu, Qinghai, Ningxia and Xinjiang)

1. Distribution of Star-rated Hotels by Numbers

In 2017, there were 1,182 star-rated hotels in northwest China, mainly two star-rated four star-rated hotels. Specifically, there are 31 five star-rated hotels, accounting for 2.62% of the total star-rated hotels in northwest China. There are 233 four star-rated hotels in total, accounting for 19.71% of the total star-rated hotels in northwest China. There are 671 three star-rated hotels in total, accounting for 56.77% of the total in northwest region. There are 242 two star-rated hotels in total, accounting for 20.47% of the total number of two star-rated hotels in northwest China. There are 5 one star-rated hotels in total, accounting for 0.42% of the total star-rated hotels in northwest China (Figure 4-56).

Compared with 2016, the proportion of five star-rated hotels decreased by 7.78%, four star-rated hotels decreased by 1.44%, three star-rated hotels decreased by 1.63%, two-star hotels increased by 6.78% and one-star hotels increased by 53.69%.

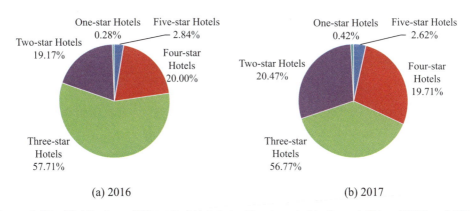

(a) 2016   (b) 2017

Figure 4-56   Distribution of Star-rated Hotels by Numbers in Northwest China (2016 and 2017)

According to the distribution of star-rated hotels, Shaanxi had 300 star-rated hotels in 2017, accounting for 25.38% of the number of star-rated hotels in northwest China. Gansu has 304 star-rated hotels, accounting for 25.72% of the star-rated hotels in northwest China. There are 162 star-rated hotels in Qinghai, accounting for 13.71% of the star-rated hotels in northwest China. Ningxia has 94 star-rated hotels, accounting for 7.95% of the star-rated hotels in northwest China. Xinjiang has 322 star-rated hotels, accounting for 27.24% of the number of star-rated hotels in northwest China.

Compared with 2016, the number of star-rated hotels in Shaanxi, Gansu, Qinghai and Ningxia increased by 25, 5, 86 and 4, respectively, with increases of 9.09%, 1.67%, 113.16% and 4.44% respectively. The number of star-rated hotels in Xinjiang decreased by 28, with a decrease of 8.00% (Figure 4-57).

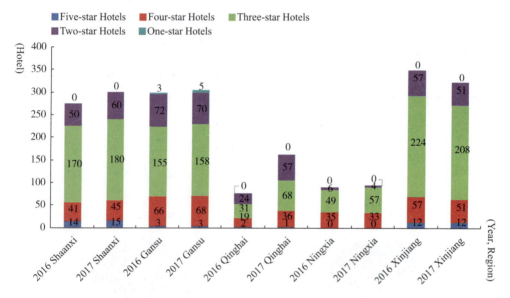

Figure 4-57　Quantity Distribution of Star-rated Hotels with Different Star Grades in Northwest China (2016 and 2017)

In terms of the distribution structure of the number of star-rated hotels, three star-rated hotels dominated the northwest region in 2017, followed by two-star, four-star, five-star and one star-rated hotels. Specifically, Shaanxi has 0, 60, 180, 45 and 15 one star-rated to five star-rated hotels, accounting for 0%, 20.00%, 60.00%, 15.00% and 5.00% of its total hotels. Gansu has 5, 70, 158, 68 and 3 one to five star-rated hotels, accounting for 1.64%, 23.03%, 51.97%, 22.37% and 0.99% of its total hotels. The number of one star-rated to five star-rated hotels in Qinghai province is 0, 57, 68, 36 and 1, accounting for 0%, 35.19%, 41.98%, 22.22% and 0.62%, respectively. The number of one star-rated to five star-rated hotels in Ningxia is 0, 4, 57, 33 and 0 respectively, accounting for 0%, 4.26%, 60.64%, 35.11% and 0% of the total number of hotels in Ningxia. The number of one star-rated to five star-rated hotels in Xinjiang is 0, 51, 208, 51 and 12 respectively, accounting for 0%, 15.84%, 64.60%, 15.84% and 3.73% respectively.

2. Distribution of Star-rated Hotels by Revenue

(1) Operational Revenue and its Composition

In 2017, the annual operational revenue of star-rated hotels in northwest China reached 11.875 billion yuan, an increase of 2.75% year-on-year, of which 5.647 billion yuan was generated from rooms, accounting for 47.56% of the operational revenue of star-rated hotels in northwest China. The food and beverage revenue was 5.021 billion yuan, accounting for 42.28% of the operational revenue of star-rated hotels in northwest China. Other revenue was 1.207 billion yuan, accounting for 10.16% of the operational revenue of star-rated hotels in northwest China.

In 2017, the operational revenue of Shaanxi, Gansu, Qinghai, Ningxia and Xinjiang was 4.753 billion yuan, 2.349 billion yuan, 821 million yuan, 822 million yuan and 3.132 billion yuan, respectively, accounting for 40.02%, 19.78%, 6.90%, 6.93% and 26.37%, among which Shaanxi accounted for the largest proportion. Compared with the same period in 2016, the operational revenue of Shaanxi, Gansu, Qinghai and Ningxia increased year-on-year, with growth rates of 13.41%, 0.48%, 22.58% and 7.87%, respectively. The operational revenue of Xinjiang decreased by 12.97% year-on-year (Figure 4-58).

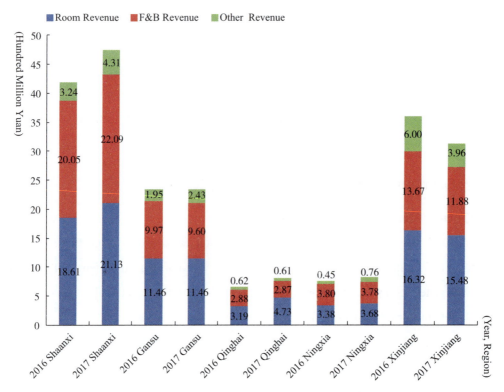

Figure 4-58   The Revenue and Composition of Star-rated Hotels in Northwest China (2016 and 2017)

In 2017, the operational revenue structure of star-rated hotels in northwest China was mainly dominated by the revenue of rooms and food and beverage, accounting for 89.84% of the total revenue. Specifically, consistent with the performance in 2016, the food and beverage revenue of Shaanxi and Ningxia star-rated hotels exceeded the room revenue, accounting for 46.48% and 45.99% of the total operational revenue respectively. The room revenue of the star-rated hotels in Gansu, Qinghai and Xinjiang all exceeded the revenue of food and beverage, accounting for 48.78%, 57.65% and 49.42% of the total operational revenue respectively (Table 4-7).

Table 4-7   The Share of Operational Revenues of Star-rated Hotels in Northwest China (2016 and 2017)

	Room Revenue (%)		Food and Beverage Revenue (%)		Other Revenue (%)	
	2016	2017	2016	2017	2016	2017
Northwest China	45.81	47.56	43.58	42.28	10.61	10.16
Shaanxi	44.42	44.46	47.85	46.48	7.73	9.07
Gansu	49.02	48.78	42.65	40.86	8.33	10.35
Qinghai	47.62	57.65	43.07	34.96	9.30	7.39
Ningxia	44.28	44.80	49.79	45.99	5.93	9.21
Xinjiang	45.33	49.42	37.98	37.92	16.68	12.66

(2) Operational Revenue of Each Hundred-Yuan Fixed Asset

In terms of the each hundred-yuan fixed assets realized by star-rated hotels, the northwestern region in 2017 reached 33.16 yuan, with a year-on-year increase of 0.71 yuan, an increase of 2.20%. Specifically, Qinghai star-rated hotel's fixed asset investment has the strongest earning capacity, which was 35.34 yuan, with a year-on-year decrease of 2.94 yuan, a decrease of 7.68%. Shaanxi reached 34.82 yuan, with a year-on-year increase of 2.20 yuan, an increase of 6.74%. Gansu reached 34.29 yuan, with a year-on-year increase of 1.60 yuan, an increase of 4.89%. Ningxia reached 32.90 yuan, with a year-on-year increase of 1.60 yuan, an increase of 5.11%. Xinjiang was 29.83 yuan, with a year-on-year decrease of 1.62 yuan, a decrease of 5.15% (Figure 4-59).

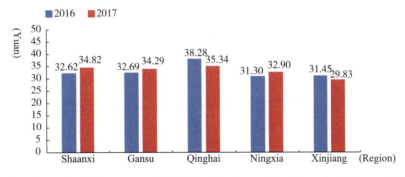

Figure 4-59   Operational Revenues of Each Hundred-yuan Fixed Assets of Star-rated Hotels in Northwest China (2016 and 2017)

(3) Operational Revenues per Room

In terms of the operational revenue per room of the star-rated hotel, northwest China was 84,000 yuan in 2017, with a year-on-year decrease of 3,100 yuan, a decrease of 3.55%. Specifically, Shaanxi was 112,400 yuan, with a year-on-year increase of 3,100 yuan, an inecrease of 3.59%. Gansu was 70,700 yuan, with a year-on-year decrease of 1,200 yuan, a decrease of 1.67%. Qinghai was 55,400 yuan, with a year-on-year decrease of 32,000 yuan, a decrease of 36.61%. Ningxia was 78,600 yuan, with a year-on-year increase of 2,200 yuan, an increase of 2.88%. Xinjiang was 76,900 yuan, with a year-on-year decrease of 4,800 yuan, a decrease of 5.88% (Figure 4-60).

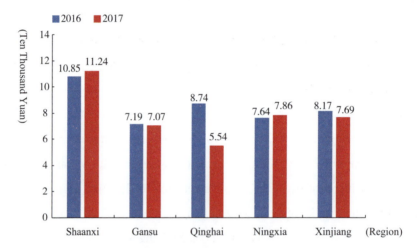

Figure 4-60   Operational Revenues of Each Room of Star-rated Hotels in Northwest China (2016 and 2017)

(4) Fixed Assets for Each Hundred-yuan Operational Revenue

In terms of the fixed assets occupied by each hundred-yuan of operational revenue of star-rated hotels, the northwest China in 2017 reached 301.61 yuan, which decreased by 6.63 yuan year-on-year, with a decrease of 2.15%. Specifically, Shaanxi was 287.22 yuan, with a year-on-year decrease of 19.38 yuan, a decrease of 6.32%. Gansu was 291.60 yuan, with a year-on-year decrease of 14.32 yuan, a decrease of 4.68%. Qinghai was 282.93 yuan, with a year-on-year increase of 21.73 yuan, an increase of 8.32%. Ningxia was 303.91 yuan, with a year-on-year decrease of 15.60 yuan, a decrease of 4.88%. Xinjiang was 335.21 yuan, with a year-on-year increase of 17.22 yuan, an increase of 5.42% (Figure 4-61).

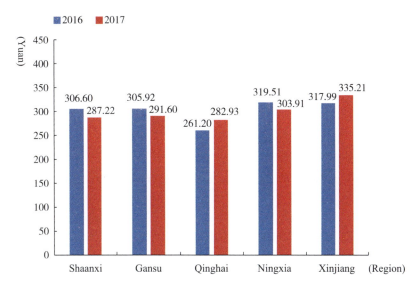

Figure 4-61   Fix Assets for Each Hundred-Yuan Operational Revenues of Star-rated Hotels in Northwest China(2016 and 2017)

3. Distribution of Star-rated Hotels by Total Profit

In terms of the annual total profit of star-rated hotels , the annual loss of northwest China in 2017 was 268 million yuan, and the year-on-year loss decreased by 648 million yuan to 70.77%. Specifically, only Shaanxi achieved weak profit in 2017, while other regions were in deficit. Shaanxi's total profit was 18 million yuan, while its year-on-year profit increased by 219 million yuan by 109.18%. Gansu lost 126 million yuan, a year-on-year increase of loss of 193 million yuan, an increase of 289.95%. Qinghai lost 9 million yuan, the year-on-year loss increased 4 million yuan, the increase was 87.43%. Ningxia suffered a loss of 25 million yuan, with a decrease of loss of 576 million yuan and a decrease of 95.80%. Xinjiang lost 126 million yuan, a decrease o floss of 50 million yuan from the previous year, a decrease of 28.31% (Figure 4-62).

Figure 4-62   Total Profits of Star-rated Hotels in Northwest China (2016 and 2017)

4. Distribution of Star-rated Hotels by Human Resources

In terms of the number of star-rated hotel employees, the northwestern region was 88,000 in 2017, with a year-on-year decrease of 8,100 and a decrease of 8.39%. Specifically, Shaanxi had 29,900 people, with a year-on-year decrease of 4,600 and a decrease of 13.33%. Gansu had 21,100 people, with a year-on-year decrease of 1,000 and a decrease of 4.52%. Qinghai was 7,500, with a year-on-year increase of 1,700 and an increase of 29.31%. Ningxia was 6,700 people, with a year-on-year decrease of 300 and a decrease of 4.29%. Xinjiang was 22,700, with a year-on-year decrease of 3,900 and a decrease of 14.66% (Figure 4-63).

In terms of the staff to room ratio of star-rated hotels, the number in northwestern China was 0.62 people per room in 2017, with a decrease of 0.10 people per room year on year, a decrease of 14.01%. Specifically, Shaanxi had 0.71 people per room, with a decrease of 0.18 people per room year on year, a decrease of 20.22%. Gansu was 0.64 people per room, with a decrease of 0.04 people per room year on year, a decrease of 5.88%. Qinghai had 0.51 people per room, with a decrease of 0.25 people per room year on year, a decrease of 32.89%. Ningxia had 0.64 people per room, with a decrease of 0.06 people per room year on year, a decrease of 8.57%. Xinjiang was 0.56 people per room, with a decrease of 0.04g people per room year on year, a decrease of 6.67%.

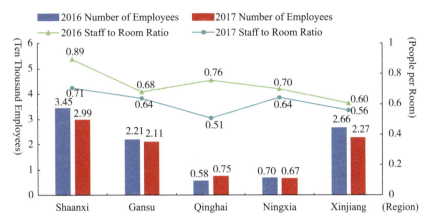

Figure 4-63   The Number of Employees and Staff to Room Ratio of Star-rated Hotels in

Northwest China (2016 and 2017)

责任编辑：谯　洁
责任印制：冯冬青
封面设计：中文天地

图书在版编目（ＣＩＰ）数据

中国星级饭店行业发展研究报告. 2018：汉英对照 /
中华人民共和国文化和旅游部市场管理司编. -- 北京 ：
中国旅游出版社，2018.12
ISBN 978-7-5032-6190-9

Ⅰ．①中… Ⅱ．①中… Ⅲ．①饭店业－经济发展－研
究报告－中国－2018－汉、英 Ⅳ．①F719.3

中国版本图书馆CIP数据核字（2019）第010590号

书　　　名：中国星级饭店行业发展研究报告 2018

作　　　者：中华人民共和国文化和旅游部市场管理司编
出版发行：中国旅游出版社
　　　　　（北京建国门内大街甲 9 号　邮编：100005 ）
　　　　　http://www.cttp.net.cn　E-mail:cttp@mct.gov.cn
　　　　　营销中心电话：010-85166503
排　　　版：北京旅教文化传播有限公司
经　　　销：全国各地新华书店
印　　　刷：北京金吉士印刷有限责任公司
版　　　次：2018 年 12 月第 1 版　2018 年 12 月第 1 次印刷
开　　　本：787 毫米 × 1092 毫米　1/16
印　　　张：13.25
字　　　数：162 千
定　　　价：68.00 元
ＩＳＢＮ　978-7-5032-6190-9